Ali Goes Walking Dot Com

Ali Allen

ISBN: 1463690096
ISBN-13: 9781463690090

DEDICATION

For Mum and Dad
xxxxxxx.

CONTENTS

ACKNOWLEDGMENTS

To Mick who accompanied me for many miles of my journey. To my sisters, Jill and Lesley who supported me along the way. To my extended family, in-laws and rediscovered cousins. To all my friends both old and the new that I met in my travels and of course to my blog followers who were with me in spirit every step of the way. To Dr Cindy and all at the Fatigue Consultation Clinic for allowing me this extended leave. To my husband Curt, who diligently stayed home with my son, making this trip possible. And to my parents, Brenda and Tony who ultimately made every thing possible............

i

1

INTRODUCTION

What is this book anyway? A guidebook to Britain? A long distance walking guide? A bizarre self-help book on how to deal with a midlife crisis or a chronic disease? A book about returning to ones roots? A dedication to my parents?

I must admit I have struggled with its identity, eventually concluding that this book is all and none of the above and I think it best for the reader to decide. Because of its diversity, I trust you will relate to it in some way and derive whatever your pleasure out of this book.

However it is, quite simply, my blog and the story of my journey that began in the middle of a sodden field in Britain 2009.

As I walked through that field towards the beautiful stately home of Chatsworth, I suddenly had this overwhelming desire to keep going, to keep walking. In that moment, all the confusion and uncertainty that I had been feeling about my father's stroke and imminent death were suddenly lost in the tangible beauty of England. Beneath its ancient oaks, I felt a wonderful sense of security and strength. I didn't care that it was pouring with rain and that I was squelching through ankle deep cow manure. I was not thinking about my Father but about how great the tea and apple cake had just tasted. I was left wondering what lay over the next gate, field and beyond. I felt extremely happy and was filled with questions about what would happen if I just kept walking. How far was I capable of walking? Suddenly everything seemed so simple and I knew I had to walk.

2

BLOG BEGINNINGS

**TESTING, TESTING
SUNDAY, MARCH 21, 2010**

This is my blog..... –
-Posted by Ali at 08:35 AM

Comments:
-Trev   21 March 2010
Excellent posting!

-AngandShawn   01 May 2010
It looks great! Now all you need to do is start walking.....Let me know
if you need any help. Click on our names to view our blog.

**CRAZY SPRING WEATHER
TUESDAY, MAY 11 2010**

I refuse to let this weather prevent me from getting in shape. I
have less than one month to go and I am far from fit. I could go to
the gym I suppose but I also need to get myself psychologically in
shape. The gym is just too comfortable of an environment. Too
tame. I need miserable. I need cold and wet if I am to truly create the
hardships I could face this summer walking across Britain. So today
was absolutely perfect.

As I rode my mountain bike 3,500 feet down canyon to work, the
snow turned to driving rain. My sunglasses proved marginally helpful

but dirty water from my fender-less bike splattered up over my already fogged lenses, road grit wedged between my teeth and a combination of both covered my clothing from head to toe. Water saturated through my pants and a steady flow trickled down into my boots, bathing my toes in a pool of icy cold water. My gloves became water logged, my fingers numb and I felt like I was trying to brake wearing a pair of boxing gloves against slick, wet tires that had no intention of stopping.

There I was barreling down the hill, dodging rock and mudslides, with very little ability to stop and zero visibility. I did survive the experience however and arrived at work far from presentable. I would like to say I enjoyed the experience but......

Yes like I said, today's training was absolutely perfect. So perfect I decided to blog about it.

-posted by Ali at 10:09 PM

Comments:

-Sarah   May 14 2010

Yes I saw you peddling away against the driving sleet. I was tempted to stop to tell you it was hailing in the valley, but no instead I sent you a text to how "hard core" you are.....way to go girl friend ☺

ORACLES AND ANTI-INFLAMMATORIES
SATURDAY, MAY 15, 2010

Had another successful training day today walking up Mount Olympus. Not THE Mount Olympus in Greece but our very own one here in Salt Lake City, Utah. Not sure of the connection but I am fairly sure you won't find a bunch of Greek gods atop this mountain but more likely the Mormon Moroni blowing his trumpet? (no offence Mormons-but I couldn't resist).

I have never understood why Americans can't make up there own names for places. For example, why would you bother to take the perilous journey across the Atlantic from Plymouth to escape a place of persecution only to name the place of arrival Plymouth as well? How utterly uncreative!

But I digress....

My husband Curt and I know this mountain very well and have climbed it several times over our 22 years here in Salt Lake. It is a good mountain for early spring, as the route is south facing and way too hot in the summer to undertake. It is not very high at just over

9000 ft but extremely steep and ascends 4,800 ft in only 3.1 miles. There is a fun scramble to the summit and once on top there are magnificent, panoramic views of the Wasatch Range and the Salt Lake Valley. Despite having to negotiate steep slippery snow, it only took us 2 1/2 hours to summit. Not bad for a couple of out-of-shape oldies. Interestingly we didn't feel our age until our knees and ankles started to creek upon descent. Gone are the days of running down to get to the pub quicker.

This seems to be the appropriate place to put a plug in for 'Chandler's Walk Shoppe'. If you are ever in Salt Lake and in need of a pair of shoes, visit Skip and he will fit you with a pair or modify any pair of shoes in the shop to fit your feet - even grotesquely disfigured feet such as mine. Today I was wearing my brand new Keen Gortex® boots kitted out with custom Skip-made inner soles. I am happy to say that they felt superbly comfortable and didn't even need braking in. My boots are incredibly important and really need to be first rate because I have a major problem. A recent CAT scan of my feet showed my feeble bones resembling holey chunks of Swiss cheese, substantially nibbled on around the edges. Even my untrained eye could tell that this was not at all normal and that my rheumatoid arthritis (RA) was having a heyday and potentially ruining my long walk planned for this summer.

Lovely Dr Rhodes gently suggested I take up an alternate sport other than running or walking, something like "water aerobics or knitting". He told me that my feet are not meant for walking.

So you see, this summit meant a lot to me today because I proved to myself that I am still capable. I won't need that swimsuit or those knitting needles, just my Keen boots and inner soles from Skip. Oh...... and handfuls of anti- inflammatories, a cortisone shot and various other pharmaceuticals.

-posted by Ali at 09:30 PM

Comments
-Curt   16 May 2010

Wow, it was a fun spring trip and the old bodies held up reasonably well. Can't wait to get to Mother England and start walking along the sea coast – and get to the pub at the end of a soggy English summer day for a fire in the corner and a pint on the table and the football world cup on the tele. Anyway here's to training for it.   Curtie xx

SPRING AT WINTERBOURNE CABIN
TUESDAY, MAY 18, 2010

Time to practice my blog writing skills....

....

It's raining outside and there's a fly buzzing around the cabin. Seems that spring has finally arrived here at Winterbourne. If I open the windows I can hear the creek flowing freely. Not long now and the noise will be deafening as the creek fills with spring melt-off and roars off down canyon.

The snow is disappearing swiftly, revealing various piles of objects (rusty old fire pits, construction debris, tools) left out, sometimes unintentionally, to over-winter. It's always fun to see the ground again and to see what does emerge from the depths of the Rocky Mountain snow.

Our meadow is also happy to be lifted of its heavy white blanket and the first green shoots are visible and poking bravely upwards, out of the winter soil and into the warming spring air. Soon others will follow suit and collectively they will become our meadow of dancing wild flowers this summer.

It's early yet and the aspen trees are still barren but look closely and the buds are present, just waiting for that perfect spring day when they will burst forth, bringing color to the landscape and shade to our cabin. The Honeycomb cliffs will then be lost from our view until the leaves fall once again in the autumn.

Soon the moose will be visiting us here again at Winterbourne, returning from their winter diaspora down canyon. The ground squirrels have already emerged from their long slumbers, playful and hungry and the birds are plentiful and happy to serenade us daily with a wonderful dawn chorus.

The ski areas are closed and the canyon is quiet. No traffic, no snow cats, no avalanche control. When the valley heats up, the people will return but until then we have the canyon to ourselves.

This is truly a wonderful time of year up here at Winterbourne Cabin in Big Cottonwood Canyon, Utah.

-posted by Ali at 06:32 PM

INTRODUCING THE IPAD
FRIDAY, MAY 21, 2010

I am very proud of myself. From a complete moron technologically, I have advanced this year considerably and can now use an Apple computer at a fairly acceptable skill level (although I am sure my 14 year old son would dispute this); I have a facebook account and have even figured out how to post things on it; I have this blog of course and I now have the very latest in technology – an iPad (no, not a feminine hygiene product Kristin!).

Introducing the 16 GB, 3G iPad.......

Excitedly I turned on this beautiful, sleek machine to write a blog and quickly encountered a problem, as I could not post or edit this blog on it. This was however resolved fairly quickly by buying their blog app (BlogPress). So far, I absolutely love this invention but it does seem a little bit of a scam, that you have to buy a whole load of *essential* 'extras', such as a case to prevent it from scratching, an additional piece of equipment to enable it to download pictures and all the Apps to make it do really cool things (or in my case to write this *essential* blog)

Pause for a sip of tea..........

The touch keyboard takes some getting used to and seems to have a mind of its own (but don't all computers?). My typing thus far has required multiple corrections for it to even resemble English. Of course this could be something to do with my arthritic stiff, sausage-shaped fingers that inevitably touch multiple keys at once. Perhaps then, it is not possible for me to get used to it? Whatever, because the one finger approach seems to working quite well.

Anyway, enough of the negative because the BIG plus is that the iPad only weighs 1 point something pounds. This is very important because I will be taking it walking with me this summer.

Yes, I *will* be walking this summer. So, for anyone who is yearning to break free from the daily treadmill of predictability, stay posted to this blog because I am off on an adventure.

-posted by Ali using from BlogPress using my iPad at 11:45 PM

THE GRAND PLAN
THURSDAY, MAY 27, 2010

I keep on alluding to a plan I have for this summer, something about a long walk? I thought it was about time I let you in on some of the details.

I am leaving work at the end of this week and fly to the UK next Thursday. Hubby, Curt doesn't have to leave work because he joined the other 10% of the US population in unemployment last November and has not worked since. Ivan, our son isn't coming at all because being fourteen, he would rather hang out at the mall with his friends (and to his credit honor his commitment to his soccer team).

"No offence mum, but why would I want to walk across England with my parents?" says Ivan

I am sure he will regret this decision but better he learn by his own mistakes than force him to come and then all of us have a miserable time. So he will be staying with friends for whom I am eternally grateful and with his cousins in California. Curt will return in five weeks but I have the whole summer to complete my goal (yes I have the most amazing, patient and understanding hubby in the entire world).

My goal then is to walk from Lands End (the furthest south west point in Britain) to John O'Groats (furthest north easterly point in Britain) - for short LEJOG - about 1000 miles depending on the route taken. I want to take the national trails, rather than roads but not sure if I can link them together. Doubtful I will complete the entire route this summer so I may have to cheat between trails with public transport or return next year.

I am sure that the many reasons for this trip will enfold as I blog, but above all I am drawn to the simplicity of donning backpack and just walking, because.....I can. As I walk I will ponder the meaning of my life, or perhaps I won't think at all. I will observe the British way of life and their odd customs from an American 'Resident Alien' perspective, absent from my mother country for the last 22 years. And I have this vision of arriving in John O'Groats a changed person (hopefully way nicer and much wiser) looking Forest Gumpish with a long grey beard.

FYI - I am trying to put a map of my route on this blog but don't hold your breath. I am not that 'techy' yet. But please note that my iPad has a GPS on it. Just discovered this. Fantastic – I think!

-posted by Ali using BlogPress from my iPad at 09:04 AM

-location E Big Cottonwood Canyon Road Cottonwood Canyon, United States

Comments:

-Amy   June 01 2010

Brilliant blog Ali! I am looking forward to following you on your journey. So exciting!! Who gets to keep Ruby while you are both gone?

Thanks. Really enjoying writing it and pleased you are reading [Ruby to Laynee and Fritz to Deb].

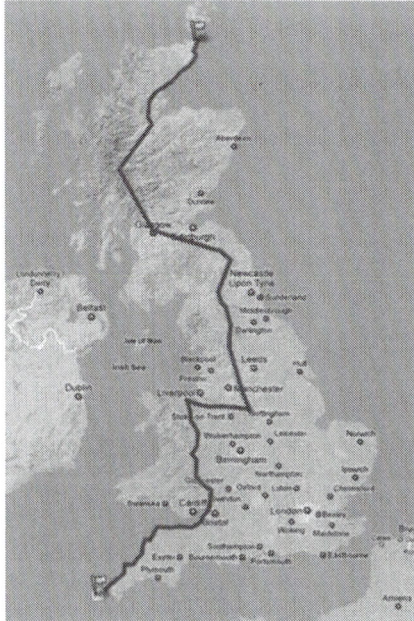

'LEJOG'
Lands End to John O'Groats
Via various National Trails

3

THE START OF A GRAND ADVENTURE

I AM HERE
FRIDAY, JUNE 04, 2010

IPad GPS has located me at the "Case is Altered Pub" in Ruislip, Middlesex, UK

I nearly didn't come. Major changes at last moment.

Despite the fact we are traveling on buddy passes (stand-by), I had stupidly not even considered that we might not get seats on the plane. We have always had such good luck with using these tickets but we have also never traveled during the busy summer months. Hence, when I checked our flights 24 hours before, there was no availability. Worse still, there was absolutely no availability on *any* flights to the UK.

Curt decided he could not come. If availability was difficult now, how he could guarantee a timely return to pick up Ivan after his stay with his cousins in California?

Parental responsibilities reigned and I started to feel really guilty. Now I was not only abandoning my son but also my husband, who was not only being far more responsible than me but also incredibly understanding of my need to do this trip. A roller coaster of emotions followed and not necessarily in the order I should have been feeling them. After guilt, came disappointment that Curt wasn't coming, then relief that he would be staying at home to take care of Ivan, then panic at the prospect of doing this all alone. Then finally denial, which allowed me transfer over our shared gear from his backpack to mine and to eventually get on the plane – to Amsterdam!

Now, I did consider throwing-in-the-towel in acceptance that this entire trip was a completely unrealistic idea. And I must admit to feeling a little bit concerned that I had bitten off more than I could chew, but I also felt a responsibility towards its completion, or at least initiation. As Deb pointed out, I have a lot of people living vicariously through this blog (in part why I decided to write one – keeps me accountable). But I also have to admit to considering the option of living incognito for the next three months, in some form of disguise and simply inventing fabulous blogs about all my adventures. Indeed I may have done this, had I thought my imagination good enough.

I did eventually reconcile (rightly or wrongly) my leaving by feeling as though I was setting an example to Ivan. Although he was not prepared to accompany me at this time, should I allow that to stop me and just give up my dream? I was showing him strength of conviction and wanted him to know that I was facing my fears, adapting as necessary. It is nice to know that he feels comfortable here in Salt Lake but I want him to know that travel is always an option and the big wide world is open for him to explore.

From Amsterdam, I ended up on British Airways flight to London City Airport. Where? Had never heard of this airport before but it took a wonderful flight path through clear blue skies, with breath taking views of London and touched down on a landing strip in what seemed like the middle of the Thames river. I had landed in the East London dockland.

-posted by Ali using BlogPress from my iPad

Comments

-Trev   June 06, 2010
I think a pub is an excellent place to begin most any adventure. And I'm sure you've figured out the iPad quirks.....keep going

-DavidHodge   June 08, 2010
Where are you now?

-Ali   June 08, 2010
Hey Trev. Haven't found clin-phone many yet but looking. Too busy walking right now xx

A light rail system took us (my extremely heavy, awkward backpack and I) through the East London docklands.

This is the side of London that is rarely visited by tourists and is a juxtaposition of old and new, grotty and cute. Out the window was a landscape of ancient warehouses amongst newly renovated lofts.

Neatly aligned terra cotta chimney pots sat atop traditional rows of tiny terraced London homes on cobbled streets, contrasting against housing projects of gross apartment buildings, cement and graffiti clad, washing strewn from door to door, surrounded by ghastly barbed wire enclosed playgrounds.

The Thames flowed to the left of the tracks, warehouses ominously gracing its banks and barges afloat its murky waters – carrying goodness knows what – but a living memory to a by-gone era when London was once the industrial capital of the world. And of course there were the Pubs, dependably situated on street corners, exteriors adorned with cheerful hanging baskets of flowing flowers and wrought iron signs distinguishing each one with fantastic names such as the 'Slug and Lettuce' and 'The Cock and Bottle'

Was that the 2012 Olympic stadium I could see under construction across the Thames?

Through the centre of London on the Tube and then northeasterly out to my childhood stomping grounds. I became very emotional as I passed through my local station and eventually alighted at Ruislip, a very familiar place. I needed that familiarity as I had a massive list of things to do.

Walking down Ruislip High Street with a large backpack on was very strange. This was still my home away from home until last year when everything changed – when my Dad passed away and my family home was sold. I now had nowhere to go. I was a 'traveler' here now.

[Ironic to think I left this place to seek adventure in far off lands and now here I was returning 22 years later with the very same backpack in search of a new adventure in my former home].

Firstly, in order to feel a little more connected with the world, I had to charge my UK mobile phone. I went into the phone shop, bought extra minutes and left it there, charging upon the counter.

Secondly, I wanted to purchase a UK data plan for my iPad so I could use it remotely and I went in to a neighboring phone shop (another reason I went to Ruislip – lots of phone shops). Unfortunately this required a UK address, which I did not have but I did leave my backpack rather conspicuously in the corner of their shop. I was beginning to buckle under the weight and surprising warmth of the unusually sunny day. And as already mentioned, I was feeling a little odd walking in a London suburb with this extraordinarily large pack adorned with walking stick, tent and various other artichokes (artichokes?) – spell check just automatically and incorrectly changed my chosen word of 'articles' to 'artichokes'. Hmm, wonder what other weird words may have gone by unnoticed?

Thirdly, I needed to send on my fridge dependent RA medications, via overnight mail, to my sister Jill, who had kindly assumed responsibility for sending them on to subsequent unknown places that I may be. So I went in to a shop called Mail Boxes but unable to do this until Monday, I left my meds in their fridge (as my gel pack had defrosted). They kindly agreed to package them up and send them Monday and in appreciation I gave them my blog address. Oh and $30 which left me penniless.

Fourthly, I went in to a shop called 'Ice Land' and deposited my gel pack amongst the frozen peas.

Once I had succeeded in spreading my belongings along Ruislip High Street, I braved the bank. I was greeted with a very long queue of people, all waiting for three very slow tellers. By this time, having lived the longest day of my life, I was extremely tired. Next in line to me was an old man, hunched over a cane and at least 100 years old but waiting patiently without complaint. I wished I had my walking stick too but it was in the phone shop, so I shuffled from foot to foot, sighing and groaning and trying to lean on the wobbly rope, there to keep us in an orderly line. And it was so damn hot in there.

I had some questions about my account before I could withdraw money. Finally it was my turn and a very unsympathetic teller told me that I had to make an appointment to ask questions and there was no availability until Tuesday. I think I experienced then, what could only be akin to an anxiety attack. My heart raced and I felt short of breath. No money until Tuesday? No money for the next four days? Luckily the other teller was a lot more sympathetic and recognized my anxiety attack. She took me aside, listened to my questions and supplied me with a phone to call my offshore account. Questions answered and money in hand I left the bank, believing that there may be a God after all. But I hate British banks.

Traveling never used to be this complicated did it? Cell phones, iPads, money, medications and symptoms related to chronic diseases all make it so much more difficult!

....

Wow, brill. Am currently, as I write this blog, on a train heading down towards Lands End and ironically the start of my walk. We have just crossed the impressive Tamar Bridge built by the famous Isambard Kingdom Brunel and have crossed the border into Cornwall. But back to London because I am not finished yet

....

So once my cell phone was charged, I could call my sister Jill. It was so wonderful to hear a familiar voice and I felt instantly better. It had only been about 30 hours since I had left Salt Lake City but it was plenty of time to question what in the hell I was doing. Sitting outside Costa coffee on Ruislip high street was one of those times and my ensuing exhaustion was making me feel very emotional. What was I to do next? Where was I staying tonight? Despite my fatigued brain I was beginning to realize that all of those questions were pointless. I was not in control of my destiny and like it or not, that was partly the intention of this trip. I was living in the moment, something I couldn't generally achieve in my 'normal' life of 30 hours ago.

Renewed by my telephone call, I gathered my belongings together and walked towards my old local pub the 'Case is Altered'. I had a few weeks ago emailed a handful of friends to meet me there, the evening of my arrival. Being so disorganized before departure, I had not confirmed this with any of them and doubted that anyone would show up. I sat in the corner of the busy pub and reminisced about many joyful evenings spent here with friends. And then last year we had come to this pub after Dad's funeral and everyone had piled in, to have a few drinks in his memory and to eat perfect little triangular white bread sandwiches, English style (Dad would have loved them!).

To my surprise, Karen suddenly appeared before me, grinning hugely and all loneliness was instantly gone. Karen had driven up 2 hours from Portsmouth without even knowing that I would be there, an old school friend that I hadn't seen for over 15 years and I can't begin to tell you how happy I was to see her. The evening took off, with more friends arriving and it couldn't have been a more perfect start to my trip.

Everyone that showed at the pub agreed that my LEJOG idea was utterly ridiculous, especially when they tried to pick up my backpack, but they all said they would support me and I felt loved and felt as though I had come home. Thank you, thank you everyone for coming. You all mean so much to me ☺

I didn't have to set up my tent on the cricket field opposite but instead spent the night in a real bed at the home of Karen's parents, Beryl and John.

See, best not to plan. It was an absolutely brilliant, spontaneous evening.

-posted by Ali using BlogPress from my iPad at 02:32AM

4

THE SOUTHWEST COASTAL PATH

DAY 1: LANDS END TO PENDEEN
SUNDAY, JUNE 06, 2010

I am sitting in the North Inn, at Pendeen, Cornwall and just finishing up with a "Tribute Premium Cornish Ale" – wish you were here Curt to share this with me.

Feeling absolutely brilliant and very proud of myself because I have completed my first day of LEJOG. After having so much difficultly just walking approximately two miles to the Case is Altered yesterday (yesterday?? – who knows?), I was seriously doubting my capabilities. My backpack is just way too heavy.

After the five-hour train journey and arriving in Penzance yesterday, I set up my tent outside Castle Horneck youth hostel and then proceeded to enjoy the excellent facilities within. A beautiful Georgian house recently remodeled with a full bar, café, lounge with TV and some great people to talk to. Finally got to talk with Curt but still have to figure out all my communications and technology, because despite eventually getting a data plan set up with Vodaphone for my iPad, I still can't get Internet access. Once I get access I will be able to publish these blogs.

This morning I took an open top bus to Lands End and the start (for me) of the South West Coastal Path (SWCP). I can honestly say I did not know if I was going to be able to walk even a mile but living in the moment, I didn't care, because the bus ride was beautiful. Had my picture taken in front of the legendary sign pointing towards John

O'Groats (874 miles) and indicating the mileage from whence I had come (SLC = 5355 miles) – cheesy but obligatory!

And then started off walking along the cliffs.

And promptly got lost.

I was map-less but presumed it would be easy enough, walking along a coastal path. My only plan was to walk from the very end of England, northeasterly, keeping the sea to my left and England to my right. Then turn right at Pendeen lighthouse and find somewhere to stay. How difficult could it be?

Pause......to pet the pub dog walking under my table. God I love pubs.

The SWCP turned out to be a well-worn path as expected but perhaps a little too well worn as there was a multitude of them to choose from. There were neat little signposts indicating the way to go when it was completely obvious and none when absolutely necessary. This drove me nuts and a wrong turn invariably meant a detour up another massive hill and eventually back down again when I caught sight of the main path meandering below me or visa versa. I never seemed to make the right choice (kind of like changing lanes in a traffic jam).

At one point I realized I was obviously following the wrong trail, when I became 'cliffed' out and was forced to bushwhack back up the cliff. I arrived at a barbed wire fence, presumably to keep people from the cliff edge that I had been walking along. It was either go all the way back or scale the fence. With an almighty heave ho, I hurled my backpack over, not in the least bit confident that I was going to be able to get my self over. But feeling very light without all that weight, I climbed over, gingerly avoiding the barbs on top and landed proudly on the other side to join my pack. However, I also joined a pack of bulls. Ten of them to be exact and located right where I needed to walk. They didn't have rings in their noses and didn't look too terribly threatening but they did all have massive pointy horns. I put my head down and tried not to make eye contact as I walked amongst them, so close I could feel them breathing on me.

Tin and copper have been mined here since the mid 1700s and ruined mines and chimneys litter the coastline. Because of this, mine shafts are everywhere and there are little signposts strewn along the path, indicating that apparently I am 'In Danger of Death'.

One very large hole in the ground had a particularly large 'Danger, Keep Out' sign and a much smaller 'Missing, have you seen me?'

sign, complete with a sad picture of that missing person. Did they think he had fallen down the shaft? Did they even look?

All this made me start to think about the implications should I fall down one of those holes and go 'missing'. Would I get one of those posters? I can only imagine all of the sightings of me that would come flooding in. "Oh yes, I saw her, she was staggering under the weight of an extraordinarily large rucksack". And "She asked me where she could get a cup of tea" or " she stopped and asked where the next ice cream van could be located" or perhaps even "she didn't seem to know where she was going, kept on back tracking, up and down, asking if she was going in the right direction"

I think I made a point of talking to everyone I passed as it made me feel better. Most people were just out for leisurely walks and not one person seemed to be doing what I was doing.

I found a refreshment stand and had the most fantastic cup of tea. Once again confirming that everything tastes better when you have to work for it.

Then ten miles and six hours later I caught sight of Pendeen lighthouse and turned right into the village.

So here I am, camped in the field next to the pub. I did it. I walked my first day and lived to tell the tale.

Tomorrow I will walk fourteen miles to St Ives and it is supposed to be the most 'challenging, rugged and remote' section of the SWCP. Tomorrow I will have a map, purchased this evening from the minute but fantastically stocked (way better than any huge supermarket in Salt Lake) village shop.

I had Twigletts and Ribena for dinner. For those of you that are not familiar with these fantastic British delicacies: Twigletts are whole-wheat baked sticks (or twigs!) covered in marmite (a black malodorous salty spread made from yeast extract and full of nutritious B vitamins); Ribena is a very sugary blackcurrant drink guaranteed to rot your teeth on contact. Did I tell you that I love this country?

Good night from my REI quarter dome tent. Wish me luck tomorrow

-posted by Ali using BlogPress from my iPad at 02:38 AM

DAY 2: PENDEEN TO ST IVES
MONDAY, JUNE 07, 2010

I woke up with the dawning day at 4:00 am and decided to start walking. Good thing, as it took me until 5:45 to get packed up and back on the trail.

I was initially unable to put any weight on my right ankle but once I put my boots back on and had worked it in a bit it miraculously improved (I am putting a lot of faith in that cortisone shot Dr Rhodes – so far so good☺).

So I set off in overcast, damp weather and it felt great. Confidently I stroke off down an unknown footpath that seemed to go in the right general direction back to the coastline and sure enough I landed right back on the SWCP. Although my shoulders felt bruised and my body generally hammered, I felt amazingly good and the weight of my pack wasn't too significant for the first 7 hours! – Comforting to think I may be getting used to the weight already.

The trail was deserted and absolutely spectacular. I did not see a soul for the first 5 hours and then only bumped in to two other couples and one solitary guy. This could be partly due to the atrocious weather that ensued. The damp mist turned into a gentle drizzle then an absolute down pour for the remainder of the day.

The first few hours were a dream come true for me. From plan conception I had romantic visions of walking along the cliff tops on the edge of Britain, at one with the wind, the sky and the ground; taking in the scenery, the nature, the smells and the history of my homeland. Well that dream had become a reality and I was immensely happy. And I wasn't just talking myself into this state; I was honestly feeling it.

I walked with and without iPod, listening to a variety of music but was most inspired by the Celtic songs that fit the scenery so perfectly and the rhythmic nature of the drums kept me striding on. I was happily belting out the lyrics to a Nora Jones song and had just got to the part "come on home and turn me on" when on the brow of a hill, I literally bumped into the solitary hiker mentioned earlier. I greeted him with an embarrassed grin but he understood that anything went up here on the cliffs and he seemed as happy to see me as I him. Coming from the opposite direction we were anxious to exchange news of the path ahead. I had been walking for about 5 hours at this point and was thinking it had been wonderful, but was ready to stop walking sooner rather than later. He told me I was half way and I felt devastated and psychologically things went down hill for me, from that point forth!

Physically there were down hills too but just as many up hills. Up and down the cliffs I walked, over bogs, rocky sections, parts where the trail was so skinny I could hardly place two feet together in it. The overgrown ferns and long grasses on either side of the skinny trail would drench me as I brushed through them. That and the pouring rain proved too much for my Gortex® jacket, boots and gaiters. I was soaked through to the bone. I wanted to stop, rest, snack, take off my pack but every time I tried, I would freeze, so it was better to keep on walking.

The iPod eventually died and instead I talked to myself, usually words of encouragement and it seemed to really help.

I even found myself talking to the signs. There were not many, so I was always glad to see them, even if they brought me bad news. Initially it would be "thank you mister signpost" but later it was "f*!!*, not another 6 miles to go". But I would make a point of pausing for a few minutes in front of the signs, brushing them off if necessary and hoping in vain they would give me more information. Not so of course, but they did tell me that I was heading in the right direction and this was useful, although I was doing so much better with route finding today anyway (probably because the trail was so much more remote and there was not a multitude of them to choose from, unlike yesterday).

There were some amusing signs. One even directed at sheep:
'NOTICE TO ALL SHEEP –
it is illegal to go beyond this point without a movement license. Failure to comply
with this law may result in a fine, imprisonment or both'.

Lots more hazard signs too, warning of impending death and private property signs warning of Adders at large instead of Doberman Pinchers and interesting signs about various ship wrecks. Guess this is entertainment when walking with one's self!

During the last few miles, I have to admit, I started to feel a little desperate. I did consider putting up my tent and spending a night out on the trail, but everything, including my tent was soaking wet. The thought of being in St Ives, warm and dry was driving me forward and I had already decided I was taking a B&B for the night.

I quickened my pace but the trail was becoming increasingly slippery and I was aware that one fall could be the end of me. Along with the signs, my walking stick had become my close friend. I had deliberated over whether to bring it, but now it was indispensable, allowing me to balance on stepping-stones crossing the bogs and helped to get me up the hills and over the rocks. But one mile from St Ives, in my frenzy to get there, the inevitable happened. I slipped and fell forwards. My shin hit hard on a pointed rock and the weight of my pack kept me pinned down. I thought something must be broken. I howled in pain and assumed I was doomed. But I saw no bones protruding form my leg and thankful of this and in sheer desperation I pretty much ran the last mile into St Ives.

St Ives – a gorgeous, picture perfect pirate town. But at this moment, all I cared about was a B&B. Despite the rain, tourists were out in hoards, paddling in the streets and chatting to each other from under umbrellas and huge bag like ponchos, like it was all completely normal.

Water poured from the roofs and drainpipes of ancient buildings, amassing into flash floods down the tiny cobble stones streets and alleyways.

I wasn't odd then, when I turned up at the tourist information centre in a pool of water, looking like I had been sitting in a bath for 10 hours with my clothes and backpack on. Although I must have looked somewhat pathetic and in need of special help, as they gave me a cup of tea, booked me a B&B and even drove me to it! The very kind lady said her daughter was currently in Chile back packing and she hoped someone would do the same for her daughter if she needed it. I assured her that good karma was coming her way.

I experienced elation and relief on a magnitude that I have never experienced before as I walked over the threshold of Porthminster bed and breakfast and was greeted by the nicest man in the world, David Hodge. He had already turned on the central heating in anticipation of the weary, bedraggled travelers arrival.

-posted by Ali using BlogPress from my iPad at 01:18 AM
-location: St Ives, United Kingdom

Comments:
-Sarah   June 10, 2010
Makes me want to join you. I bet a cuppa tea has never tasted SO great.

TECHNOLOGY PROBLEMS TUESDAY, JUNE 08, 2010

Finally! Internet access. What a hassle this is proving to be.

You are going to have to be patient with me regarding postings because without a working 3G data plan, I am dependent on wifi and this iPad does not seem to pick up signals very easily.

I have a feeling that blogs will be posted in chunks because there may be periods without any Internet access.

Now off to Truro to try and sort out my data plan.

Comments:
-stromqui   June 08,2010
Hi Ali,
I'm following and happy for you. It looks beautiful
Don S.

-Anonymous   June 08,2010
Hi Ali!!
Great to be able to track you and your thoughts like this! Just wanted you to know we are thinking of you. Keep smiling.
Lol Mel and the Eggs x

-Trev   June 09, 2010
Did you see the man with seven wives? (That's all I know about St. Ives).

-LL Wright   June 09, 2010
I'm really loving your blog – it's like I get to experience England vicariously through you! The pictures are awesome. What beautiful scenery.

DAY 3: ST IVES TO GWITHIAN WEDNESDAY, JUNE 09 2010

This morning, I left my new home at Porthminster and strode out once more into the unknown.

But not before I had enjoyed the massive vegetarian breakfast and an entire French press of coffee - my first cup of coffee for a few days and for those of you that know me well, this is quite significant!

The weather yesterday was actually beautiful but I decided to stay another day in St Ives and try to get a little more sorted – I was feeling as though I had been on the go since I had left Salt Lake. I ended up taking a bus back to Pendeen to collect my all important plug adapter and mobile phone charger that I had left in the North Inn. I could not understand how I could have possibly left them in the pub, as I was being especially careful, knowing that these items are the key to my connectivity with the rest of the world. But anyway despite this I had left them plugged into the wall.

Interesting to travel via bus the section of the trail that I had slogged along the day before. I thought it would minimize the achievement for me but actually it still seemed a bloody long way! Funny to think though that I had felt so alone and remote, when actually, the road had never been too far away.

Anyway, here I was on the coastal path again and glad of it. Why was this feeling so good? Before leaving, the other guests had all taken a turn to pick up my backpack and had all wondered how I was possibly walking with it and I had no answer for them. It hurt at first to put it back on and it was a painful reminder of the day before but once walking I was thankfully able to overcome this discomfort. My body is dealing amazingly well with all this abuse.

I followed along side the beautiful stretches of sandy beaches, through dense vegetation, on a very well defined path. Then over a golf course, through an ancient churchyard and the middle of a funeral, along the A30, around the estuary, across the oldest draw bridge in Britain. It was so much more civilized than the previous days hikes but somewhat difficult to navigate. I frequently stopped to ask directions and got very complicated answers "go along here, turn left, turn right, through the housing estate, over the bridge, dip through the hedge, you can't miss it". I was always very proud when I would look up at just the right time to see the minuscule acorn sign (for the SWCP) pointing through the hedge, to make that all important "dip through" to join the official trail once again.

I reached Hayle with relative ease. I had initially planned to stop here but feeling good, I decided to carry on just a few more miles to a campsite. It seems as though 6 miles has become my limit of comfort. After that, it all becomes so much more difficult. I found the next 4 miles very hard and the pack once again felt unbearable. I had the choice of either walking across sand dunes and cliffs or walking along the beach. I decided on the latter but the tide was not out all the way. I had to remove my boots and paddle through sections until those sections became too deep with crashing waves and then I had to climb back up onto the cliffs and dunes

I was especially excited to get to Gwithians because I was meeting up with my good friend Chris, who had driven down from Plymouth to see me. I met Chris 24 years ago when I was 19 years old, living in Plymouth, unemployed and a rock climber.

He reminded me of all the climbs we had done together and I did not realize that I walked right by some of them the other day, on route to St Ives. He had brought an old Devon and Cornwall climbing guide and pointed out our names in print, the new route we had put up together in 1987.

Climbing and me seem a long time ago now. My arthritic fingers and feet would make it impossible for me to climb and anyway, I have a major fear of heights now. As for Chris, he is still climbing, better that he ever has. He has overcome a terrible illness and is still an extreme climber – most impressive. We spent a wonderful evening together, watching the sun set over Godvery island and lighthouse (supposedly the inspiration for Virginia Woolf's novel 'To the Lighthouse'), reminiscing and finding out that we have the same opinion on many different philosophical issues. For instance we both have chronic diseases but have decided not to sit and wait for them to progress, but to live life to it's fullest. I am very aware that this walk may make my RA worse but I am not about to sit around and wait until I am incapable of walking.

Thanks Chris for coming

-posted by Ali using BlogPress from my iPad at 09:15 AM

-Location: Chynance, Portreath, United Kingdom

Comments:

-Sarah   June 12, 2010

OMG that breakfast looks delicious!!

-Amy   June 12, 2010

What a fantastic adventure!! Just remember to be easy on yourself when things get tough.. you can take all the public transport you like because its about the journey. Things don't always end up looking the way you expected them to. So proud of you!! And a wee bit jealous too. XOXO

DAY 4: GWITHIAN TO PORTREATH
THURSDAY, JUNE 10, 2010

The tent is flapping like crazy. I can hear the waves crashing on the rocks below and I have to admit I am feeling, not scared but definitely out of my comfort zone. It's my first night of 'wild' camping and it does feel pretty wild to me. I am up on the cliff tops, just outside of Portreath.

I only walked 6 miles today. When I arrived in Portreath I found a great café with free wifi posted on the window and I ended up staying there all afternoon, checking emails, looking at Face book etc. It didn't seem like there was anywhere good to camp and because it wasn't raining, I didn't want to do a B&B. I have a new rule (one that I am sure to break) – if it is raining, I can get a B&B but then not eat out and if it isn't raining I have to camp and then I can treat myself to eating out. This will keep the cost down a little.

So with lack of campsites and feeling as though I hadn't done that much today (as remember 6 miles is now a piece of cake for me) I decided to walk out of town and camp up on the cliffs. I went to the nearest 'cost cutter' my new favorite shop and bought some noodles to cook up for dinner. I also thought it was about time I used the stove and pots I have been carrying around with me. I finally got a gas canister for the stove the other day but I was unsure if it was the right one and hadn't wanted to cause an explosion (could this happen with the wrong gas?) in Porthminster B&B as I had liked it there too much! So anyway I asked Chris to check it out last night and it didn't explode. Sorry Chris to make you do this!

I struggled up the cliff with a bag of food and full bottle of water to add to my load. Couldn't find anywhere appropriate to camp. Those perfectly mowed flat areas I had been seeing along my route so far, and noted as so perfect for camping, were nowhere to be found. All I could find were steep, lumpy banks of gorse, heather and thistles. There was a flat area I considered but it was very close to the cliff edge and it was awfully windy. I had visions of the wind picking up the tent in the middle of the night, while I slumbered on inside and acting as a parachute, it would float gently down to the sea below. I would awake as the cold Atlantic entered my sleeping bag and in a confused, panicked state I would drown, trapped in my REI quarter dome tent that had become my coffin in the sea.

Wow have I got an active imagination tonight.

Anyway, didn't camp there. Jumped the little stone wall instead and I am camped in a farmers field. Now I am worried that a crazed farmer will beat me to death in the middle of the night or stick his pitchfork in me, finally tipped over the edge by another illegal camper in his field. Or perhaps another herd of bulls (this time with rings in their noses and big pointy horns) will stampede my tent in the night.

Enough of that but it is weird how the nighttime can bring these thoughts upon us. Do guys have these thoughts when they are alone or is it just us women? I just wish the tent would stop flapping. It's unnerving.

So I turned on the stove, ready to cook my noodles but it was sitting on uneven ground in long grass and I felt a little uncomfortable when the blades of grass started to ignite. So I scrapped dinner and ate the avocado sandwich Chris had so kindly made me in an effort to improve my diet and supplemented that with salted peanuts and a Star Bar (I really love these).

Now I am considering taking a sleeping pill pilfered from the sample cupboard at work (perks of working in a medical clinic!). I need to sleep well tonight as I have a big day tomorrow. I really hope it doesn't rain.

If I go missing, don't bother looking down the mine shafts, I will be floating on the sea in my green and orange REI tent.

-posted by Ali using BlogPress from my iPad at 09:57 AM

DAY 5: PORTHREATH TO PERRANPORTH
FRIDAY, JUNE 11, 2010

The "Upper Deck" pub is filling up and getting very raucous. My stomach is full of veggie lasagna and filling up with my second pint of Doom Bar.

Feeling great, considering how awful I felt when I arrived at Perranporth about noon today.

Left the farmers field at 5:00 this morning and got started on the path early. I was very aware that I was moving slowly and blisters were forming on my feet. I changed my socks yesterday, which was probably a mistake. I seem to do better with thin liner socks; anything else rucks up inside my boots.

I am now sporting a multitude of different shaped plasters (Band-Aids) of varying thicknesses all over my toes. My worst blisters are on the bottom of my toes and not sure how to best dress those. My big toe nails are both black and blue. This could be a real problem.

Yesterday the SWCP had been like a road running along the top of the cliff and today it was pretty similar but more up and down, as it dipped down into coves and backup again. The weather was fantastic with beautiful blue skies but cool enough to wear a smart wool layer.

Today was a little bit of walk down memory lane for me. Most of our early family holidays took place in Wales. Unlike most London families we would spend our summer holidays not on the beach, but climbing mountains in Wales. I first went up Snowdon (highest peak in Wales) at age five. This was my introduction to the mountains and instilled within me a deep love for them. Anyway, when I was about thirteen (I suppose Mum would have been about my age now), Mum decided she no longer wanted to walk and we joined the masses of holidaymakers on the beaches of Cornwall. We then spent our time at these beaches that I was walking over today.

I walked down into Chappel Porth cove and saw up the hill, the cottage I had stayed in with Sharon and her family. Then tried to spot the cave that my sister Jill and I had sheltered in during a big thunderstorm in the mid 80's. For some reason this occasion was significant enough for me to remember. In the cave was a mother with her child and she was showing the little girl how to make a fire and light it. Jill and I were both very impressed with this and agreed that when we had children we would bring them up just like this.

Of course when you have children it is never that easy. They come into this world with a personality all of there own and often any preconceived ideas on how to raise them are not realistic. I've done my best to raise Ivan in this vein but not without a struggle. I don't think I have ever been in a cave with him however.....

Things are getting wilder in this pub by the minute. Every one is dancing, clapping, stomping their feet and singing, 'You're a wanker' – a particularly charming song! Just realized that it's Friday night. Which means tomorrow is Saturday 12th, which also means that England v U.S. World Cup match is on.

I had better get back to my tent and get some sleep, so I can get to my next destination tomorrow in time to watch the game.

So let me quickly finish off about today.

The route finding was really pretty obvious but I think I have also become SWCP savvy. I am in synch with the path and can now generally recognize which path I should take – weird. I also take short cuts whenever possible and recognized one today when I saw the tide was out in one of the coves and rather than go up and over the cliff I went over the beach. It was a little tricky, as the rocks were covered in slippery seaweed and scary sea creatures – so once again, my walking stick came in handy to steady me. The path generally followed spectacular cliff edges with sheer rock faces plummeting down to the sea. Remote rocky coves and caves lay far below, a haven for by-gone smugglers to stash their pirated loot.

As I turned the corner and saw Perranaporth beach stretched before me, I started to cry. Have absolutely no reason why, other than the fact I was exhausted, my feet were killing me and I was listening to a particularly stirring rendition of Amazing Grace by Susan Boyle (I know, a little embarrassing to admit but she does have a fantastic voice) on my iPod. That is the last time I remember having my iPod. I think I have lost it and I am gutted. I feel as though I have lost a friend and I am not sure how I will do without it. It must have fallen out of my pocket

I have got a cold and I never get colds. Better get some sleep now.

-posted by Ali using BlogPress from my iPad at 11:12 AM

-Location: Beach Rd, United Kingdom

Comments:

DAY 6: WORLD CUP – PERRANPORTH TO CRANTOCK
SATURDAY, JUNE 12, 2010

Guess what? Found my iPod when packing up my stuff this morning. Yippee.

More the same today i.e. cliffs, beaches, coves, rocks; all wonderfully spectacular of course.

Walking along the beach, although very tempting to avoid the cliffs, is really hard for me. It is monotonous, tough on my feet, I sink in the sand and basically it seems never ending. Surprisingly I do better on the ups and downs of the cliffs. As I looked back at my miles of solitary footprints I couldn't help but be reminded of this poem learnt during my very brief, 'born again Christian period', at age 16!

FOOT STEPS IN THE SAND

One night I dreamed I was walking along the beach with my Lord. Many scenes from my life flashed across the sky.

In each scene I noticed footprints in the sand. Sometimes there were two sets of footprints, other times there was one only.....Mary Stevenson, 1936

It felt hard from the beginning again today. I was not particularly motivated to get up and go and when I did, it hurt all over. One too many beers last night and I definitely have cold. I need to do better at re-hydrating – I just looked at my face and it is looking a little wrinkly. I don't have Curt here to remind me to drink.

So I stopped for a coffee (I know Curt, it's a diuretic) in a pub conveniently located right on the trail but it was closed. I sulked and he made me a coffee. I walked on towards Newquay but on the way, I stopped and talked to a couple who suggested this would not be a good place on a Saturday night, especially a 'World Cup' Saturday night. "Too many drunks and yobs" they said. They recommended a pub up on the hill and a campsite not far. I had to back track a little but it sounded like a good idea. I had to ensure a good pub for the match tonight.

I checked in at the pub first and no wifi, but plugs galore, a couple of TVs, plenty of England flags and a fantastic location atop the cliffs overlooking the bay. I had reached the beautiful village of Crantock. After refueling with a cheesy baguette and confirming the time of the game tonight, I went in search of the campsite. I passed by a wooden shack and outside a bearded fellow sat with a beautiful Retriever by his side. Of course I stopped to pet the dog and saw that he was busy cleaning an old radio. He explained that he fixes gramophones and proudly showed me his shack full of antiquarian stereos in various states of disrepair. I told him I had been trying to find someone like him for years, as we had an old Wurlitzer in Salt Lake that I would love to get working again. He gave me all sorts of advice on who to contact regarding this and I thought it was amusing that I had to come all the way here to this little village in Cornwall to gather this information. I also found out some very useful trivia about the village. Apparently it is in the Guinness book of Records for bale pushing. Bale pushing? Yes, in 2006 the village held its second annual "big bale push" This involved the locals pushing tightly packed straw cylinders around the village. And I guess they were good at it.

I walked on down the hill and saw before me the most perfect campsite yet, nestled in a green valley above a lovely sandy cove and named "Polly Joke". I was later to learn that this cove is entirely surrounded by national Trust land and has remained unchanged for centuries.

I am back in the pub now, just waiting for this evening's festivities to begin. This entire country has gone patriotic which is highly unusual. Only football, the national game (and world wars) can bring England together as one nation. The St Georges cross is flying everywhere and even went up over Downing Street this morning. This country has been gripped by world cup fever and I am right here with them; and how perfect that the first match is against the USA.

Now back in my tent and the game is over. A very amicable score of 1:1 but of course common knowledge by the time this blog goes to press. To watch the game, I sat squeezed on a couch with four other women and could not avoid getting caught up in their enthusiasm as they downed more cocktails and became increasingly verbal and boisterous. The atmosphere in the pub was perfect, with lots of oh's and ah's, cheers and boos and kids and adults alike dressed in England football attire. The draw was obviously disappointing but the English are used to disappointments. They like to support their team whole-heartedly but have very little faith they will win! The English should stick to wars as they seem to have better overall outcomes.

After the game I talked to a lot of people in the pub and gave out my blog address (people seem to be interested and this makes me very happy!), received many tips such as sewing cotton through blisters, honey on digestive biscuits to boost my calories and of course lots of water (Curt – I have really tried with this today and have not drunk any beer)

I don't have cotton for my blisters but I did just do some minor surgery to pop them and lets hope this works for tomorrow. Still feeling sick with my cold.

-posted by Ali using BlogPress from my iPad at 11:30 AM

Comments:

Linda -   June 13, 2010
Ali, I'm sitting at my IMAC catching up on all six days of your adventure. What am I to make of this: you running w/bulls, seeing old boy friends, connecting w/wonderful geezers, showing off you battered feet, sleeping at the cliffs' edge, guzzling up the pints, seeing Britain's coast as it has been seen for the eons. You write like the best of your countrymen. I am onboard w/you, and feel as if I am along for the adventure

Love, Linda

-Anonymous   June 14, 2010
Loving hearing all about it (is that English?!). I've heard about cotton
for blisters – in fact am going to tell Madeline our eldest about it –
she has just returned from a hiking weekend for the Duke of
Edinburgh award and has a lot blisters apparently! Hope you're
getting good weather today – gorgeous down in Portsmouth! R xx (as
in Rachel F!)

-Amy   June 14, 2010
Veggie lasagna in a British pub! Happy to know you are getting all
kinds of veggie options. Talked to Benny the other day...things are
looking up. Sent him the link to your blog as well. Must feel good
knowing we all wait for the next one to post. I am living vicariously
☺

-Sarah   June 14, 2010
I feel like I'm along for the rip Ali while reading you blog, except I
don't have the blisters and everything I eat and drink goes to my
waist! One of these days I AM going to walk "across England". I'll
keep trying to call you and maybe one of these days I'll get through.

-AngandShawn   June 15, 2010
Hey Ali, I so wish I could see the sights and views that you are
seeing. Please upload as many pictures as possible. I want to go to
England so badly. I really believe I should have been born in
England. Even though I am a die hard U.S. soccer fan right now.
Shawn.

-Trev   June 15, 2010
you might want to try witch hazel on your feet @ night if you can
find any – theoretically it helps you skin get tougher and less blister-y.
(I'm enjoying the ride too – got Joyce hooked today as well) –t

DAY 7: CRANTOCK TO TREYARNON
SUNDAY, JUNE 13, 2010
"Set out into the unknown and the universe will take care of you"
    That is what Tim said today and I believe him.
    Tim was my knight in shining armour (wet suit – and please notice
my more frequent use of English spellings) and I his damsel in
distress.

I was stuck on the banks of the Gannel tidal estuary. Yesterday it had been a big beach to walk across but this morning it was a massive body of water. There was supposed to be a ferry and a footbridge but there were no signs of either. I had followed the coastal path to where it entered the water with a signpost pointing across it to Newquay. There I sat to ponder this perplexing situation.

'Mar not my face, but let me be, Safe in this lone cavern by the sea, Let the waves around me roar, Kissing my lips for ever more'
[inscription below a carving of a woman's face in the rocks]

It wasn't long before Tim paddled around the corner and into my life, on his horse disguised as a paddle board. I shouted across to him and waved madly. He shouted back, agreeing that I was indeed stuck and at the mercy of the tide but....he offered me a lift over.

Unable to believe my amazing luck, I sat on the paddle board with my pack balancing on the front and crossed my fingers that we wouldn't capsize. I wasn't concerned for my own safety but for all my gadgets and electronics contained within my pack, for sure ruined if we tipped into the Gannel. But my knight in a wet suit swam gallantly across the Gannel, steadily pushing the paddle board and delivered all of me safely to the other side.

Tim was not only my rescuer but also a lovely, wise human who provided therapy (something I am always in need of), practiced meditation and Tai chi and was a wealth of psychological support for me. Amazingly enough he went out with a girl from Ogden, had skied the Cottonwood Canyons and knew Utah very well – as ever, such a small world.

I learnt that my blisters were more about my psychological state and that something was out of balance (true – my pack has made me completely out of balance for the last seven days and I often think I am chemically imbalanced). My bunions that were formed in the womb meant I never really wanted to come into this world and that if I took charge of my life and not rely on other people they would go away. To rid myself of my bunions had not been a goal of this trip but hey, I'll take it! I learnt that it was a twelve-moon year and that hopefully meant better weather than the thirteen moon years. Good news all-round really. We agreed that if you can accept the worst-case scenario in your life, then life becomes easy. The key is acceptance.

Tim also provided me with a cup of tea; a guide book for the coastal path (what a novel idea!); filtered water for my bottle, recommending I sip every ten minutes (this would avoid the constant need to pee caused by chugging water); a nutritious fruit bar; a book, "the Alchemist" to read and then drove me to the other side of Newquay (I am not a purist so I don't consider this cheating), to avoid the walk through town. Also, I left a pile of now unwanted gear (stove, billies, knife, fork, compass – how do you use that thing anyway?- various clothes) with him to send back to my sister, Jill.

I was renewed by this perfectly wonderful and timely encounter, and felt sure that the universe was taking extremely good care of me. I walked with a skip in my step and a smile on my face; and laughed out loud when I stopped to pee on the path and Tom Waits, via my iPod, with such perfect timing, sang "don't get caught with you drawers down'.

The beautiful weather turned to rain for about an hour in the afternoon and justified my stay at Treyarnon youth hostel. I had met a couple of ladies on the path, Ros and Jean and ended bunking down in their dorm. They (especially Ros) were die hard SWCP ramblers and they tried desperately to organize me, going over maps, explaining that I must take into consideration not only the mileage but the total elevations for the day before embarking on my next trek. But I was awfully tired and to be honest I don't want to know what is ahead of me, else I may decide not to do it. No, here's to spontaneity. It has worked well for me thus far. Hence, I ignored all their advice, went to bed early and slept wonderfully in my cosy bunk bed.

-posted by Ali using blogPress from my iPad

DAY 8: TREYARNON TO PADSTOW
MONDAY, JUNE 14, 2010

Now where am I?

It seems the universe is still taking care of me. I am on a sailing boat, moored in Padstow harbour. I have spent a wonderful evening with Marilyn and Dave, the owners, had a fantastic home cooked meal comprising of organic farm grown veggies, a gin and tonic and now have my very own deluxe berth in the bow of the "Freyja".

How can this be happening to me? I feel the luckiest person in the world right now. To think I nearly opted out of this trip...

I cannot go on any longer without saying how much I love the British people. I had assumed that my rosy coloured view of my homeland may be shattered by this trip but it has been quite the reverse. Britain is everything I thought it to be and more. I can't believe I have only been here a week and can say this with all certainty.

Such a small country but with such diversity, all crammed in to make it so user friendly. It is a country made for walkers where towns are conveniently located within walking distance from each other. And the British people are out in it, walking dogs, eating ice creams and seemingly 'there' to assist in any way possible. The pace of life is slow (down here anyway) and apart from the walking convenience aspect, nothing else is convenient and refreshingly so. Everyone just accepts that cell phone coverage is sketchy and often non existent; the shops and information tourist boards will close just as you arrive at the door; it will be sunny one minute and pouring with rain the next; hot and cold water come out of different taps; fridges are too small and ice is unavailable.

I had thought the English people as cynical, as always complaining, but even that notion has now been thwarted - every Brit I have talked to thus far appreciate Britain for the same reasons as I.

I learnt a new word today, 'Grockles', a Cornish word for tourist. There were Grockles galore today as I approached Padstow and almost had the queue to get into this gorgeous and traditional seaside port (and of course the British love to queue) - Grockles sitting on benches, eating ice creams, languishing outside pubs, drinking beer, eating Cornish pasties, buying buckets and spades. It is quite a shock to be around so many people again after the hours of solitude on the path.

Also, a strange thing happened today. Someone stopped ME and asked ME for directions. I must be fitting in with the landscape now and looking like I belong here. In fact that's exactly how I also met my hosts, Dave and Marilyn, they were out walking and stopped me to see if I had a map. I didn't of course, but never the less, we got chatting and before the end of the conversation I had been invited back to their boat for the night.

I am not sure I would receive this kind of hospitality anywhere else in the world. I picked such a good place to have my mid life crisis ☺
-posted by Ali using BlogPress from my iPad at 02:33 AM
-location: Bude, United Kingdom

DAY 9: PADSTOW TO PORT ISSAC
TUESDAY, JUNE 15, 2010

I really enjoyed my stay on the Freyja and entered into some lively conversations last night (especially after the G&T) on all sorts of topics, such as:

Faeries and knockers:

Faery is the olde way of spelling fairy. Legend has it that faeries used to be men going around on horses, absconding fair maidens and then taking them down to the bottom of the sea where they became mermaids.

> *"Come live by the brave moon*
> *That pulls the strong tide*
> *Climb up on my horse love*
> *And be my sweet bride"*

Of course Cornwall is rife with folklore. Looking up faeries on the Internet just brought up images of the typical fairy, called a Piskie here in Cornwall. These creatures are small, prankish, laughing and heel kicking, usually good spirited and like to pick their noses. The Knockers (and I am not referring to large mammary glands) are special Piskies that live down the tin mines and would warn (by knocking) the miners of danger.

Personally I prefer the male faeries on horses – or paddle boards!!

Cornish Pasties:

"It was once said that the Devil would not dare to cross the river Tamar into Cornwall for fear of ending up as a filling in a Cornish Pasty"

Cornish pasties go back centuries, when miner's wives would pack their husband up a pasty for lunch (when wives used to take care of their husbands rather than gallivanting around the world with a back pack). It was a hearty meal usually filled with beef and potatoes. The big crust around the edge acted as a handle so they could hold onto the pasty with their dirty hands and then throw the crust to the Knockers.

No Dig Gardening:

This type of gardening has a name but I can't remember it right now, anyway Marilyn is an expert at it.

The idea is, you don't dig but continue to lay down mulch in varying thicknesses (dependent on the size of the plant) on top of the soil and allow the worms to take it on down. Everyone is happy because the microorganisms remain undisturbed, the worms don't get chopped in half by a spade and for me, no digging seems way less work. The mulch keeps the soil cool and moist and can be anything from weed free garden clippings, to leaves, grass clippings, cardboard or even cotton T shirts. Or for that matter my current socks as they are well on their way to mulch.

I left on the ferry over the Camel estuary (unfortunately no Tim necessary this time) from Padstow to Rock after going to Rick Steins for breakfast. Guess he is a famous TV chef over here (a Gordon Ramsey) and I had been hearing about his café from various people.

The ferry ride was short but beautiful and offered great views of the 'Doom Bar', a bar of sand at the entry to the estuary and responsible for many shipwrecks. Apparently the mermaid of Padstow created this doom bar and being a little upset about something (forgotten what) lured ships onto it. But more importantly, Curt's favourite beer is named after this 'Doom Bar' and had he been here, we would be taking a diversion to their brewery in Rock to celebrate his birthday. Happy Birthday yesterday, Curt....[Really wishing that Curt were here now and feeling a little guilty that he is not here to experience this with me]

I walked for a few hours enjoying the absolutely beautiful weather and then stopped to eat my Cornish pasty (veggie of course). After lunch, I was sprawled out over the path in my usual exhausted way when Mike came along and almost tripped over me.

Mike was the first person I had met so far, that was going my way. Most people are out walking small sections of the SWCP, a few are going long distances but all are going in the opposite direction. So with a common destination-Port Isaac-it was natural that we walk together.

[Mike is traveling light, doing bed and breakfasts and sending his bag on to his next destination].

Once at Port Isaac, I set up my tent in "Annie's field" and felt like I had arrived at "Old MacDonald's Farm" with chicken clucking, peacocks screeching (and boy do they), sheep bah-ing and cows a mooing. At one point a cockerel came nosing around in my tent. I then went back up to the village to have dinner and drinks with Mike at his B&B, "The Crows Nest".

-posted by Ali using BlogPress from my iPad at 02:32 AM
-location: Bude, United Kingdom

DAY 10: PORT ISAAC TO TINTAGEL
WEDNESDAY, JUNE 16, 2010

I am currently staying at the Tintagel youth hostel and have now walked 111 miles along the coast of Cornwall.

I cannot believe I have actually walked this far. Twelve days ago I left Salt Lake and in that time I have been to Amsterdam, London, Lands End and have walked 111 miles. That seems a hell of a long way for someone that had difficulty walking a couple of miles.

Now I have a guidebook (courtesy of Knight), I have been reading some information about the SWCP. The official path is actually 613 miles long and goes from Minehead to Poole. Nearly all guidebooks show it from this direction, so I guess I am doing it the wrong way round. And of course, I started more than half the way round at Lands End.

The origins of the path lie in Cornwall's smuggling history. By the early nineteenth century smuggling had become so rife that in 1822 HM Coastguard was formed to patrol the entire British coastline. A coast-hugging footpath was created to enable the coastguards to see into every cove, inlet and creek and slowly but surely law and order prevailed and the smuggling decreased. By the beginning of the twentieth century the foot patrols had been abandoned. In 1973 the Cornwall cost path was officially opened. It is England's longest national trail.

I walked all day today without my pack and it felt absolutely wonderful. I sent it on to this youth hostel with Mike's bag and we ended walking together again today. The guidebook notes this part of the trail as one of the hardest with lots of ascents and descents but without my pack, this nine mile stretch was easy. My back and my feet really enjoyed a break from all that weight.

Having a walking partner other than my shadow is a nice experience. Mike is English but has been living in Victoria, Vancouver Island, for the last 30 odd years and his mission this summer is similar to mine. It's especially nice because Mike reminds me of my dad. And although Dad's spirit has been with me every step of the way, it is nice to feel his physical presence through Mike.

We never ran out of things to talk about. He is into Chinese medicine and Chi Gong and after stopping for a pint of extremely potent cider in Trebarwith Strand, he told me a particularly funny story about a time when he was on a meditation course on a small island close to his home.....

They were meditating and conjuring up "soul bodies". After the meditation, the participants were asked to disclose their different types of soul bodies to the class. There were beautiful women, angels, wise old men, etc, and then there was Mikes...a Chinese man....but on top of his head! Problem being it would not go away and this Chinese man was still present, on top of his head, when he returned to his IT job the next day! Having no prior experience with soul bodies, he had to call the course director to ask advice on how to 'unconjure' this soul body. Apparently this apparition still returns from time to time to sit on his head but luckily it is a source of comfort to Mike.

When I arrived at the youth hostel earlier today, my pack was waiting for me and my RA meds were in the fridge – Jill had successfully sent them on. I really can't believe how this is all working out so well.

-posted by Ali using BlogPress form my iPad at 02:36 AM

DAY 11: TINTAGEL TO CRACKINGTON ON HAVEN
THURSDAY, JUNE 17, 2010

Tintagel youth hostel is in a beautiful location on the cliff edge and I saw no reason to venture out of it last night. I purchased dinner from the tiny hostel shop (pasta with a terrible packaged sauce) and from the hostel grounds I watched a beautiful sunset over the Atlantic. (I have been so incredibly lucky with the weather so far). Without even blogging I convened to my bunk early, to try and get to sleep. "Try" is the key word here as my circadian rhythms are in tune with the days and the days are awfully long here at this time of year. I am unable to sleep until the sun dips around 10:30 pm and awake every morning at sunrise at 4:30.

Legend has it that King Arthur was conceived and born in Tintagel and the remains of his castle are still here. Problem is, this castle was built in the 13th century, which post dates King Arthur by many centuries (but supposedly there is the remains of a Celtic monastery close by which could date back to his birth). It was here that the legends of Merlin, Sir Lancelot, The knight's of the Round Table, Camelot and the Holy Grail etc began to take shape and have been written about and expanded on ever since.

I was going to strike off on my own again today but the thought of carrying my backpack was not a desirable one and anyway, walking with Mike had been fun yesterday. So I left the hostel and walked over to Mike's B&B. My pack was once again transported with his and we spent another day in each other's company.

It seemed like a leisurely walk and we stopped for a long lunch in Boscastle, site of the 2004 floods. The flood swept away many buildings including a historic 13th century tearoom. Luckily they had cleverly rebuilt an identical one (complete with bowing walls and sinking roof line) so that we could enjoy a cup of tea in it.

I was just carrying my little daypack, with rain stuff and the only weight came from our lunch - the two massive Cornish pasties.

Crackington Haven was a tiny seaside hamlet with only one pub, which was also the B&B. Mike stayed there for the night and at dusk I set up my tent close by and wished I was staying inside.

-posted by ali using BlogPress from my iPad at 02:37 AM

Comments:
-LLWright   June 19 2010
Those Cornish pasties sound fabulous. I wonder want kind of "soul body" is perched on my head? I bet is weighs 500 lbs!

-linda   June 20, 2010
Ali, I just marvel at your daily experiences and the pals, guardian angels and knights you are meeting along the way. If Curt and Ivan were not here – I'm not a bit convinced you would leave England and return. And who knew there was such an entertaining, vivid writer lurking about inside you

-stromqui   June 24, 2010
I'm enjoying your posts very much and still really happy for you. Like Linda says, you're a wonderful writer.

DAY 12: CRACKINGTON HAVEN TO UPTON
FRIDAY, JUNE 18, 2010

Awoke at 4:30 and had to make the same decision about striking out on my own. Lets see, I could get on the trail early, walk alone with my heavy pack and remain clueless of my destination until I arrived. Or I could stay here for a few more hours, have breakfast in the pub, walk with Mike, not carry my pack, stay in his next B&B and have a bed for the night.

I decided on the latter.

At breakfast we picked up a couple more lost souls. We sat around the breakfast table, all four of us on a quest to find answers to our happiness. Amazingly, (although I should no longer be surprised by anything) we were in the company of another Ali, walking for a few days and finding solace along the coastal path – a successful treatment for her depression. And then Andy, down here for a few days, on a retreat from Oxford and at a cross roads with some life decisions, hoping that some time alone will provide the answers.

The path seemed different today. The cliffs are now less rugged and often thickly vegetated down to the sea. Inland the countryside appears more rolling, agricultural with greener, tamed fields and grazing animals.

On top of the cliffs, 'my' path continues to meander. Mike has a map and GPS and continually stops to check his location and confirm our direction. I on the other hand, without such tools have learnt to 'read' the path and seem to instinctively know where it goes or if I have strayed. I am very happy to know that it is possible for me to develop a new sensory skill at this age and confirms to me that modern technologies have only served to take us away from our natural capabilities and instincts. It is so fun to tap back into these primeval human skills. I have always been in awe of those stories of dogs that travel thousands of miles back to their homes, when lost and now I am beginning to understand a little better how that may be possible.

Mike and I make a good team. He has a fantastic sense of humour and regales me with nonstop funny stories about his life. He is also an avid reader with a wealth of knowledge on just about every subject. So I consider him my teacher and in turn I lead him along the path with my intuitive beacon!

But more importantly both the USA and England were playing world cup games today and we needed to get to a pub.

USA was playing early so we stopped at the only pub along the way at Widemouth. Andy, now needing some company and seeing Mike as a guru in the field of Chi Gong (something he is interested in pursuing), joined us via automobile. USA unfortunately drew again but we had a pleasing meal and drinks before Andy drove us about a mile to our next B&B.

Apparently I am Celtic in origin because my second toe is longer than my big toe. Both Andy and Mike agreed that I was like Queen Boudicca. I had a pleasing visual of me as a gladiator with long golden locks, brandishing my spear atop a chariot, leading the Celts to victory against the Romans. Yes, I like this association very much and will remember this when my confidence wanes.

We all decided to stay at the B&B for the night as it was splendid. A quintessential English B&B with ducks, geese, Shetland ponies and Alpaca's that looked like overgrown poodles. There were TVs in every room and in the lounge where we watched the next match, England v Algeria.

Mike even had a bath in his room but it was more like an extra large sink, perfect for Cornish Pixies or Knockers. My room had a shower with a poorly placed step that I stubbed my toe on without fail every time I entered the bathroom. All rooms had kettles, with a selection of coffees, tea and hot chocolate so as you can imagine, I was in my element.

I want this place, I have decided. Found out it was for sale for a mere 1.2 million pounds. Perhaps not this place then, but I would love to have a small holding, be self-sufficient and quite fancy the idea of a B&B. I will have to talk seriously to Curt about this.

-posted by Ali using BlogPress from my iPad at 10:09 AM

DAY 13: UPTON TO MORWENSTOW
SATURDAY, JUNE 19, 2010

Today while walking, I learnt all about the battle of Agincourt. Have already forgotten the important details but it was something to do with Henry 5th and England v France. Apparently the French had a cunning plan to cut off the middle finger of all the Brits so they could no longer pull their long bows. So, when the Brits were eventually victorious they went around making the V sign to all the French, proudly displaying that they still had their bow pulling fingers; hence the origin of the V sign or 'the Finger'.

Also learnt about the Battle of Waterloo, Napoleon (bloody French again) v Wellington. The best story here, was the exchange that occurred between Wellington and Lord Uxbridge after a cannon ball had blasted off Uxbridge's leg:

Uxbridge: "By God, sir, I've lost my leg!" Wellington: "By God, sir, so you have!"

With that Wellington road off on his horse leaving this poor bloke. But apparently he survived and they even saved his leg which he buried in his garden with a tomb stone and shrine, inscribed "here lies the leg......" and people would actually come and pay respects to his leg.

While on this subject, I found this quote on the Internet which I thought was pretty funny.....

Just after the Surgeon had taken off the Earls leg, Sir Hussey Vivian came into the cottage where the operation was performed "Ah Vivian!" said the wounded noble, "I want you to do me a favour. Some of my friends here seem to think I might have kept that leg on. Just go and cast your eye upon it, and tell me what you think." "I went accordingly," said Sir Hussey, "and, taking up the lacerated limb, carefully examined it, and so far as I could tell, it was completely spoiled for work. A rusty grape-shot had gone through and shattered the bones all to pieces. I therefore returned to the Marquis and told him he could set his mind quite at rest, as his leg, in my opinion, was better off than on."

No wonder the British have a reputation for the 'stiff upper lip' and it brings to mind a sketch from Ivan's favourite Monty Python movie, the 'Holy Grail'. John Cleese, (an armour clad Knight) is losing his limbs at an alarming rate but continues to fight, exclaiming that his injuries are only 'mere flesh wounds'.

Filled with all these stories of valiant English heroes and gory battles we, (yes, still with Mike) marched into Morwenstow.

Morwenstow consists of a church, a tearoom, a couple of dairy farms and a fantastic 13th century pub. In the ancient interiors of the pub, sat next to the fire, was Stanley, a wonderful Staffordshire terrier with his very own stiff upper lip – a Harelip. His shiny black lip stuck up and joined his black crusty nose to reveal his cute and crooked front teeth. Being partial to dogs with disabilities and missing my own one-eyed dog Ruby, I instantly fell in love with Stanley and his very unusual Harelip.

-posted by Ali using BlogPress from my iPad at 05:51 PM
-location:Bartwood lane, Weston Under Penyard, United Kingdom

DAY 14: MOWENSTOW TO HARTLAND QUAY
SUNDAY, JUNE 20, 2010

Joined Mike for breakfast in the Old Farm House B&B. I had camped outside on their beautifully manicured lawn. The breakfast room was surrounded by book shelves that stood on old flagstone floors under low bowing ceilings with blackened beams. Where there weren't books there were photographs of famous political figures and over breakfast we found out that our host had been bodyguard to Margaret Thatcher's successor, John Major.

Upon leaving the farmhouse, we didn't get very far as the Old Rectory Tearooms beckoned. Despite having just completed breakfast we could not resist sampling a Cream Tea. Living up to their fantastic write-up in this month's addition of 'County Living' magazine, we were served up delicious homemade scones, jam and tea and sat outside, amongst the colourful flowers of the cottage garden, enjoying the glorious sunshine.

We also had to explore the village church which was, even back in 1296, referred to as 'an old and well-known structure'; before once again joining the SWCP.

Today along the path, two simple wooden signs marked our departure from Cornwall and arrival into Devon. It was a momentous moment for me because it signified that I was actually making headway and going 'somewhere'.

On top of the cliffs we came across a curious little hut, with a solitary old table and chair, boxes full of poetry books and an information board on the wall explaining that this hut had once belonged to Ronald Duncan, playwright and poet (1914-82). He had spent many years up here in solitude composing poetry, inspired by the beauty and tortuous coast that he overlooked. Disturbing the cobwebs and dust, we positioned the table in front of the window (as we had assumed Ronald Duncan would have done) and, in between fits of giggles, Mike (being an amateur dramatic), began to recite poems as I filmed on.

We eventually arrived at our destination, Hartland Quay, a funky little place, composing of two rows of white washed buildings leading down to the harbor. The buildings housed a pub, a shipwreck museum, a gift shop and the old time hotel that I had decided to stay in. The hotel was oddly spread out, with long, amiss corridors, musty smells, weird décor and no room 3 or 13 because they are apparently considered unlucky. I felt extremely lucky however because my room had a bath.

-posted by Ali using BlogPress at 5:57 PM

DAY 15: HARTLAND QUAY TO MORTEHOE
SATURDAY, JUNE 26, 2010

This is a big day for this little island with the start of Wimbledon and the summer solstice.

While the masses descend upon Wimbledon to eat strawberries and cream and converge upon Stonehenge to participate in pagan rituals, I decide to take a bus.

It was hard saying goodbye to Mike after sharing so much with him over the last few days but it was also exciting to be off on my own again.

I turned away from the coastal path and headed inland towards the village of Hartland. I found myself on a deserted country road lined with hedgerows and trees that formed a pleasing shady tunnel. It wound steeply through sleepy hamlets, with thatched cottages and ancient churches. I was once again in awe of this beautiful country, drenched in history and simplicity. No strip malls and no 'big box' chain stores; no Home Depot, no Mac Donalds, no Office Max – ah bliss.

An intriguing bridge led to a 12th century abbey but unfortunately I didn't have time to explore. I was on a mission to catch a bus. Not that I knew what time it left.

As luck would have it (yet again), I turned up at the bus stop just in time to catch the 10:15 to Bideford. It was such a treat to be on a bus and a Double-decker bus at that. This mass of metal and diesel wound its way along the country roads, scraping just below the tunnel of trees and frequently backed up to let cars traveling in the opposite direction pass. It was a very friendly bus and all the passengers seemed to know each other and through their conversations I garnered a snap shot into their lives. Ethel and Rose were making their weekly trip to the garden centre and George was going to the bakery. At that moment their predictable lives contrasted sharply with the unpredictability of mine. I felt strangely comforted to know that life was going on as usual without me but I also felt a sense of relief that I was not 'them', doing the every-day stuff that 'they' were doing!

At Bideford I caught another bus to Barnstable and there I waited in the station café for Mick to arrive.

Mick has been a friend of mine for the last 25 years. For many of those years we have been out of touch but we have always managed to find each other again and now he has bravely agreed to join me on the path for a few days.

While trying to establish a plan of action, Mick quickly discovered that we were without guidebooks or maps for the next section of the path. Mick had made a last minute decision to leave his at home, thinking that I had a guide. Unfortunately my 'Knight-guide' inconveniently stopped at Bude. This was fine with me, but it made Mick twitch ever so slightly; maps are a guy-thing. But as I have said before I find them over rated.

Welcome to my world Mick!

We took the bus to Croye, located the SWCP and started walking. It was about 5 miles before we reached another beautiful village called Mortehoe, with an absolutely vertical hill to conquer before reaching a pub perfectly situated on top.

-posted by Ali using BlogPress from my iPad at 06:04PM

Comments:

-Trev   June 29, 2010

It looks lovely. The ClinPhone man says "hi" – have you found him yet.

Keep writing!

-linda   June 30, 2010

I like to let days go by so that when I finally stop to catch up on Ali's doings, I have a few days worth. Love you Lass.

DAY 16 – 18: MORTEHOE TO MINEHEAD
TUESDAY, JUNE 22 – JUNE 24, 2010

Major bummer. I screwed up again and tried to post some more blogs but I must have been kicked off the Internet at just the wrong time. It seems these blogs are now lost forever in cyber space, somewhere between BlogPress and Internet. This makes me very sad. But I will try and recreate them and condense as I am getting very behind.

It took Mick and I three more days to reach Minehead and the official end of the SWCP.

Day 16 we walked from Mortehoe to Coombe Martin across moorland, along the coastal reaches of Exmoor national park and up Great Hangman, the highest point along the coastal path. Dramatic high cliffs with wooded valleys contrasted with the low vegetation of the heather and moorland grasses. Scenery reminiscent of Lorna Doone and other such romantic novels.

Now, Mick initially took issue at the (in his words),"wiggly monkey" nature of the coastal path. After purchasing an OS map, he began to plot short cuts, avoiding the headlands and potentially cutting miles off our route. However after I suggested that this the whole point of the path, he quickly succumbed to the inevitable wigglyness and sublime nature of the coastal path.

Walking with Mick is a different experience again. He brings familiarity and therefore a sense of security. I have to admit that although I enjoy the excitement of being alone and all that it brings, I am happy at this point to take a back seat, enjoy Mick's company and his marvelously quirky sense of humor.

Unlike Mike (it seems as though you have to be named Michael to walk with me) he doesn't keep me entertained with constant chatter but when he does say something it is invariably hilarious. His brain works in mysterious ways, constantly making the most obscure associations, voicing them with impeccable timing and perverse use of words and often breaking out in a perfect song to match the occasion. He really makes me laugh.

Day 17 we walked from Coombe Martin to Lynton over more cliffs and moorlands, often sharing the trail with wild ponies until we ended up at a brilliant bed and breakfast. Brilliant because all the rest of them were full and brilliant because on arrival we were provided with a pot of tea and a large plate of half covered chocolate digestive biscuits and ginger nuts.

Day 18 we walked to Porlock Weir. After more cliffs and such we entered the ancient woodlands of Culbone. We seemed to walk for miles, sheltered beneath the oaks and cooled by the dampness and gentle water falls that trickled amongst them and flowed down to meet the sea.

These woods led us to the most beautiful church I have ever seen. In fact my words cannot adequately describe the beauty of this church, said to be the smallest intact parish in the country. The pews seat only 33 worshipers and services are still held regularly by candlelight. You really have to sit in it, feel its coolness, smell it and hear its silence to fully appreciate and experience the wonder of this little church.

As with most churches, a centuries old sacred Yew tree grows in the churchyard, signifying that this was once a place of pagan worship. Tilted graves lie under the tree, names obscured by time and creeping mosses but forever to remain amongst the Buttercups, Daisies and unkempt grasses of Culbone church.

Once in Porlock, after having walked 14 miles or so, we decided to take a bus to Minehead. It was another 5 miles to reach Minehead and we had heard that this section of the trail was a little boring and anyway the bus was already waiting there at the bus stop. We then waited patiently for the missing driver. Obligingly the missing driver, followed by a bunch of middle-aged tipsy women, piled out of the pub opposite and loudly boarded our bus. We then experienced a very interesting drive down the skinny lane to Minehead. Our bus squeezed past cars attempting to travel in the other direction as our jovial driver and the bunch of tipsy women, affectionately swore and banged on the windows at the terrified "bloody tourists" stuck between the bus and hedgerows.

We are now at Minehead, a seaside town, home to Butlins (a bizarre part of British culture to be expanded upon later) and a major metropolis to us. It also has a curry house.

I think I have now walked about 200 miles but I will confirm this at a later date when I have added it all up.

Off for a curry now, to celebrate and to stuff my face with popodums, veggie masala, aloo gogi (spellings?), naan breads and big beers.......

Oh and just to let you know that I am extremely happy☺
-posted by Ali using BlogPress from my iPad

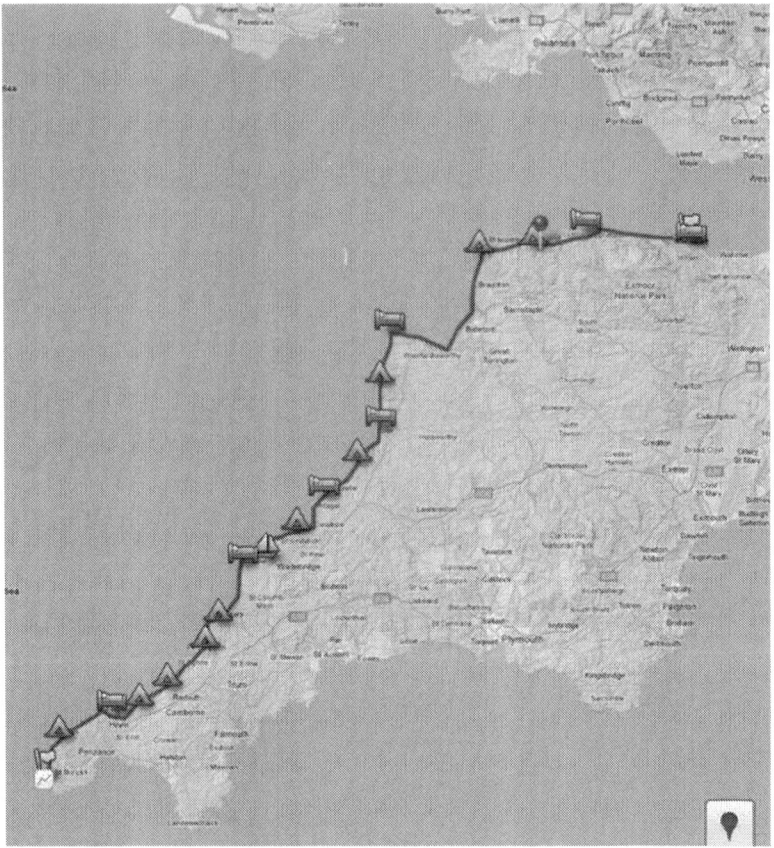

The South West Coastal Path

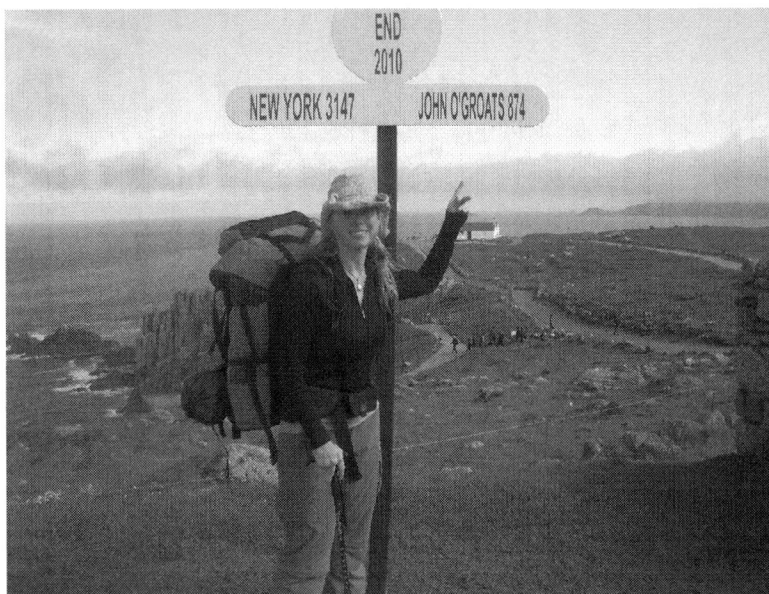

Day One - Lands End - Only 874 miles to go

The magnificent, rugged and tortuous Cornish coast

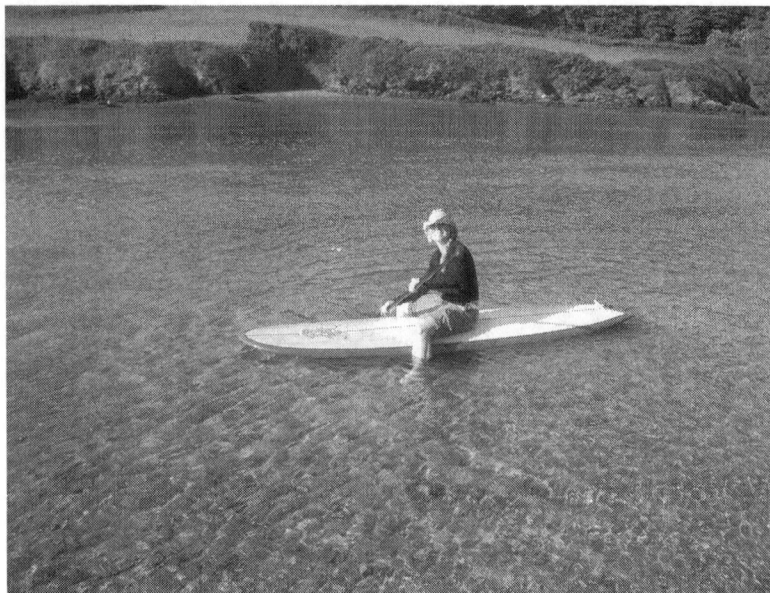

Traveling in style across the Gannel Estuary

Aboard the "Freyja" in Padstow Harbour

Happy days on the "Wiggly-monkey" Southwest Coastal Path

Culbone church – charming and spiritual

5

OFFA'S DYKE – PART ONE

DAY 19: MINEHEAD TO CHEPSTOW
SUNDAY, JULY 25, 2010

After walking for 18 straight days, I decided it was time for a day off. Being at the end of the coastal path anyway, it was necessary to find transport to my next national trail. I have decided that my next trail shall be Offa's Dyke, which will take me north along the border of England and Wales.

Took a stream train this morning. It followed the coast for a while passing campsites full of static caravans (English equivalent of a mobile home and popular to rent out for holidays) and Speedo clad holidaymakers, waving madly at the train as we chugged by. Something about a steam train that just makes people want to wave at it. Probably because it travels at such a perfect pace and makes wonderfully pleasing chugs and whistles.

The tranquility and antiquity of the steam train contrasted sharply with our next bus ride. The bus was full of families and their luggage, returning from Butlins Holiday Camp. Butlins is an institution over here and I am embarrassed to admit that even our family holidayed there once. Not sure if has changed over the years but back then, it was all about rides for the kids, knobbly knee competitions, gurning contests for those without teeth and endless evening entertainment given by Tom Jones wanna-be's. Disneyland the British way I suppose. I felt kind of emotional as I left behind the SWCP and headed towards Chepstow and the start of my next challenge.

Lessons so far from Mick: old lady flabby arms are called bingo wings; exclamation marks should not be used because most things in life are not worth such emphasis; it is not British to get excited and I should show restraint upon finding out the B&B has veggie sausages; I shouldn't worry about my genetic disposition to Alzheimer's and my current difficulty with word finding because nouns can be easily replaced with "big-elly, bog-elly, thing-y monkey"; however when describing how you are feeling you must use the Queen's English and say "very fine thank you very much", as "feeling good" is not acceptable.

I have also learnt that Mick gets very grouchy without regular intervals of tea, so we have to make sure these are scheduled into our day.

So, after a Grande Latte for me and a cup of tea for Mick in Chepstow, we headed out in search of Mrs Potts farm.

Mrs Potts was offering a field to camp in, evening meals and breakfast. This sounded delightful and gave us visions of a wonderfully plump farmer's wife with pots for hands, clanking away as she cooked us up wonderful culinary delights. This kept us focused and happy initially but our packs were heavy, it was hot and humid and our old map did not match in anyway what we were experiencing; we became easily frustrated when we could not find this campsite. The locals were not in the least bit helpful, as they had not heard of any camping in the area and when we eventually arrived at the farm, Mrs Potts was decidedly absent. But we set up camp in her field anyway, next to big pile of silage and instead of culinary delights we suffered cuppa soups and stale rolls. Despite this, Mick kindly decided he would send Mrs Potts some Brillo pads anyway, as a thank you for camping in her field.

-posted by Ali using BlogPress from my iPad at 12:34PM

Comments:

-LLWright   July 12, 2010

Remind me to tell you all about the gurning contest I was in once next time I see you in person. (Has to be seen for full effect).

-Ali   July 13, 2010

OMG can't wait to see you gurn!!

DAY 20: CHEPSTOW TO MONMOUTH
SATURDAY, JUNE26, 2010

This was to be our first day on the Offa's dyke trail. We had a schedule today and I was very excited. We were meeting my sister Jill at lunchtime to receive my next dose of medications and more importantly my first opportunity to see my sister, brother-in-law and little niece. Climbing out of Chepstow was beautiful as we hugged the cliffs overlooking the River Wye and started to walk along the actual dyke; time for a little history lesson......

Offa's Dyke was constructed by King Offa, the powerful Anglo-Saxon King of Mercia, in the 8th century and follows the border of England and Wales. Back then it was an earthen mound about 30 feet high with a deep ditch and was intended to keep the Welsh out of his kingdom. The national trail follows this dyke from the Severn estuary to Prestatyn in North Wales. It is still visible now, but only in sections and even then it is not obvious as it is nowhere near that high anymore and is usually hidden beneath dense vegetation and trees. The path is about 170 miles in length and passes through the border villages, constantly weaving in and out of Wales and England; a landscape dominated by castles and rife with stories of battles, hero's, myths and dragons.

Wales has survived against all odds. Despite a constant struggle through hundreds of years of attempted invasions, Wales (Cymru in Welsh) has maintained its identity and the Welsh their Celtic language. However Wales did eventually become under the sway of the English crown and in 1282, when the death of Llywelyn the Last, led to the conquest of the Principality of Wales by Edward the 1st of England. Since then the heir apparent to the English monarch has borne the title "Prince of Wales". Wales became part of the Kingdom of Britain in 1707 and the United Kingdom in 1801. We continued to walk through the woods with occasional tantalizing views of the River Wye far below, until we got to the rocks of the Devil's Pulpit and got a fantastic view of Tintern Abbey on the banks of the Wye. So named because the devil is supposed to have preached to the monks in an attempt to divert them from their calling.

We walked on down to the Abbey where we were to meet my sister and her family.

After a tearful reunion, we shared a picnic in the car park of Tintern Abbey (abbey went completely unappreciated), whilst I told stories of my exploits so far and tried to put into words just how fantastic I was feeling.

As my sister lives in Ross-on-Wye and not too far away, it was suggested that we come back and stay with them but I was nervous about becoming too cosy there and decided it was probably better to keep on moving. We also have a reunion planned shortly and knew I would see them again very soon.

We walked on towards Monmouth, getting a little lost and frustrated along the way until we found a pub. Refueling on a beer and Twigletts gave us just enough energy to walk on, along the hot and sticky river path to Monmouth.

Tired and hot after having walked a total of 15 miles we arrived in Monmouth and couldn't find anywhere to stay. The campsite was north and out of town a few miles, so this was not an option. The only beds left available in town were in a Mexican restaurant. Not wanting burritos for pillows and now unable to resist the idea of cosy at Jill's, we gave them a ring. Within 15 minutes we were in their car, within 30 minutes we were eating veggie burgers and drinking wickedly strong Belgian beers.

I cannot for the life of me think why I nearly passed up this opportunity to stay with my sister.

-posted by Ali using BlogPress from my iPad at 01:09PM

Comments:
-DavidHodge   July 12, 2010
Hi Ali, it was King Henry V111 who Annexed Wales to England with laws in 1536-1543. The act of Union of England and Wales with Scotland in 1707 created the United Kingdom. I do read you adventure with interest. David

-Ali   July 14, 2010
Hi David. Glad you are reading. I have come a long way since St Ives. Thanks for the corrections. Guess you can't believe everything on the Internet.

AT JILL'S
SUNDAY, JUNE 27, 2010

It was so cosy at Jill's that I couldn't bear to leave and it felt right to stay another day. My body needed a day of proper rest and it was not hard to persuade Mick of this.

The true meaning of home comforts is really apparent when they have been missing for even a short period of time. It felt so wonderful to laze around on the couch, put my feet up, put a load of clothes in the washing machine, make my latte in the morning, watch TV or use the Internet at my leisure and above all be with my family.

I also wanted to stay for the annual village fete. Bill Bryson in his little video clip on my facebook page mentions these wonderful events of British village culture and I had been trying to explain them to Curt before I left. Now I had the opportunity to experience one and take some pictures back for Curt.

Jill and Steve live in Herefordshire on the border of south Wales, close to Ross-on-Wye, in a little village called Weston Under Penyard. Their centuries old stone cottage sits on Ponts Hill surrounded by a beautiful English garden.

Edie is my gorgeous niece, almost two and extremely special in many ways.

The village fete was everything and more than expected. The village vicar was in attendance, proudly reading out the grand prize raffle winners over the loud speaker. There were races for the children, stalls with tombolas, tin can targets, lucky dips, hoopla, skittles, guess the bear's birthday, cake and bakes etc, etc; all this while the brass band merrily played on in the back ground providing a wonderful atmosphere. So glad to know these wonderfully simple and quintessentially English events still exist.

So, there you are Curt, that's your typical English fete.

'In England, we relax by guessing the weight of a pig, throwing a ring over a far of chutney and thinking it's wonderful if it's not raining"
By Miles Kington

By 3:00 pm the fete was clearing out because of the World Cup. We cleared out too and watched England lose disappointingly to Germany 4:1.

That is it then, the end of the world cup for both the USA and England.

We spent the rest of the evening drinking those wickedly strong Belgian beers again, looking at pictures and ended up with Jill and I having a cry and reminiscing about Dad.

-posted by Ali using BlogPress from my iPad at 01:40PM

Comments:

-stromqui   July 13, 2010

I am really enjoying your posts-so colorful, so much fun to hear your responses to you familiar places. And fun to see you visit your niece.

I'm glad you're doing it. Hope you are feeling well. Don S.

-mike   July 13, 2010
Sounds like all is still going well as I too sit on the couch watch the telly – and get used to Canada again.
Thought you might find this interesting.
http;//www.landsendjhonogroats.info/walking_tips/map.h tml

-Ali   July 14, 2010
Thanks for your comments. I have been responding but they don't seem to be posting. Signed in another way so we will see if this works. Don S, so glad you are following and yes, I am feeling very well.

DAY 21: MONMOUTH TO PANDY
MONDAY, JUNE 28, 2010

We packed up and said goodbye knowing that I would be seeing Jill, Steve and Edie again very soon.

Steve drove us back into Monmouth and we headed north through farmers fields, over stiles and through more farmers fields, down country lanes over more stiles and farmers fields. This went on for miles and we didn't see a soul.

We had stupidly forgotten to pack a lunch and we were therefore depending on passing by a perfect pub to provide us with refreshments.

When we eventually met up with two hikers coming the other way, we asked them about these expected pubs. They had come from Pandy, our destination and were much further along the route than us. They were carrying very small daypacks and told us that we would not be finding anything open until we got to Pandy.

We decided to ignore this couple; they *obviously* had by- passed the pubs without noticing. They *obviously* had delicious lunches contained within their miniscule daypacks and we didn't like at all, the way they seemed to relish the fact that we would not be finding any refreshments for the rest of our long journey.

So, we continued to fantasize about large cups of tea, cheese and pickle baguettes and packets of crisps.

The first hopeful village that we approached with PH (public house marked on OS map) had a building on the corner that looked distinctly pub-like but was lacking any signs and looked worryingly like a house. Sure enough as we stood on the corner staring in worried disbelief at this building, the only car of the day came by and confirmed our fears; this was indeed just a house. But the lady informed us that there was another pub, the Hogs Head "about a mile... no half a mile...no a mile... down the road to the right... no on the left, they might serve a cup of tea, they do functions for weddings." A trifle confusing but we consulted the map and the Offa's Dyke path went close to where we assumed she was directing us, so we set off in pursuit of the Hogs Head.

FYI – One knows that one shouldn't get too excited about the promises of a pub and the endless refreshment possibilities that it would provide but in reality one can think of nothing else until it is reached.

I also know from experience not to take directions and distances from well meaning locals too seriously, as they are invariably wrong but again, one lives in hope.

After miles down this road the Hogs Head was of course closed. We sat by the pub and chewed gloomily on a few dried apricots and dates.

Our next false hope was a shack that looked very much like a tea shack but it was instead full of souvenirs for the White Castle. Castle? Fixated entirely on the shack meant I had not even noticed the gigantic castle located next door. The shack lady informed us that she doesn't sell many souvenirs and most people (and there are not many that pass by this lonely place) hope for tea.

Then why, oh why, doesn't she dump the souvenirs and sell tea and snacks? I went on about this for the next hour or so.

Another grievance and favourite topic of conversation for us, was the utter stupidity of the guidebook Mick had purchased for this trail. In our minds (and therefore all other Dykers) it should have contained useful information on where to purchase tea along the way, accommodation and pubs. The description of the walk should have directed us via major features like castles and churches. Instead the book preferred to guide by flowers and birds; turn right at the Dandelion and left at the next Buttercup where you may be lucky enough to 'see a heron rising from the river'. The author confused us by referring to trickling streams as "babbling rivers" and waffled on about the history of incredibly boring things. Who bloody cares?

What about a cup of tea?

We passed through yet another village whose fantastic 13th

century pub was also closed on Mondays (and let me just add, unmentioned in the guide).

But all was well in the end, as 16 miles later (probably my longest day thus far) we ended up at a brilliant pub called The Old Pandy. We arrived just as the doors were opening and it had a wonderful bunk house specifically catering to outdoor enthusiasts such as ourselves, great beers, yummy food and a knowledgeable publican on the Offa' Dyke trail, called Alan.

The moral of this blog is....Make sure you take along a packed lunch otherwise ones blog is in danger of becoming incredibly boring and fixated on tea and snacks.

-posted by Ali using BlogPress from my iPad at 10:32

Comments:

-linda   July 17, 2010

Shame on those walkers you passed early on that infamous day of no packed lunch. Surely they could have shared a bite with you. After all, even if you had grandiose dreams of surely finding food and drink before Pandy, they had the skinny. So, if you come across lunch less walkers, give them a bite.

-Ali   July 17, 2010

Hell no!!

DAY 22: PANDY TO HAY-ON-WYE
TUESDAY, JUNE 29. 2010

The Old Pandy made us both a wonderful lunch today! And we strode off across the Brecon Beacons National park and up into the Black Mountains.

It was initially a tough climb out of Pandy, then miles of walking across the ridge tops with panoramic views of England and Wales, stretched out in all directions. As far as the eye could see, no large town or cities, just hamlets, villages and church steeples, nestled amongst undulating fields and copses. Amazing, that on such a densely populated island, there is still so much unpopulated countryside and that you can still feel isolated on an island, approximately the same size as Utah but containing 63 million more people. We can walk for miles and not see a soul, walk down roads and not see a car.

The Black Mountains are aptly named. Today, shadows fell over their masses, creating a darkness that blurred the line between mountain and stormy sky. They were ominous and heavy, yet soft and hazy, with dreamy wild horses galloping across their ridges.

We walked on across the endless dreamy ridge top for hours, hypnotized by the skylark's song that seemed to lull us to sleep. A flagstone path marked our way along the ridge and over the bog. It stretched for miles into the distance and as we put one foot in front in front of the other, I found my eyes closing and wondered if it was actually possible to fall asleep while walking.

Our day ended at Hay-on-Wye, the literary capital of Britain and home to numerous wonderful second hand book shops; and another castle.Mick and I were both happy here as the B&B was 'continental' style, with a self serve kitchen and an endless supply of tea bags for Mick, Landlord Beer (a Mick favourite) at the local pub and for me, Wifi.

DAY 23: HAY-ON-WYE TO GLADESTRY
WEDNESDAY, JUNE 30, 2010

More beautiful sultry, black hills today, breathtaking views, more skylarks making us sleepy, endless fields to walk through, stiles to climb over, gates to open and close, nettles to sting our legs and wheat to get stuck in our socks.

The best thing about today though, was St Mary's Church

Apparently Charles 2nd (won't attempt to guess what year he reigned) once traveled this way and was given refuge and snacks within this church. St Mary's has continued on with this tradition, providing refreshments to Dyker's and other travelers alike. A humble sign in the churchyard directed us in for 'free drinks and refreshments' and we of course decided to take full advantage of their kind offerings.

A table in the nave, next to the ancient font provided a kettle, jugs of water, hot chocolate, tea bags, instant coffee, milk and Tupperware containers of Jammy Dodgers and Custard Creams. We sat down on the pews to enjoy our treats and became the newest guests to enter our names into the visitor's book. An inscription on one of the windows read quite aptly

'Friend where for art thou come'.

I imagined how it would have been when King Charles visited all those years ago (before he got his head chopped off, or was that Charles 1st?) and I am sure the church has changed very little, although the snacks perhaps varied slightly for him.

Before leaving I left a small donation in the church box with a big thank you and wondered why more churches didn't engage in this kind of thing. Perhaps religion would have a resurgence in this country?

Ten miles later and my feet were killing me, so we decided to cut the day short in a tiny village called Gladestry, as it had a pub with accommodation available.

We watched Wimbledon and Andy Murray lost, once again putting England out of winning anything.

But I had a brilliant veggie chili over a jacket potato.

-posted by Ali using BlogPress from my iPad at 08:29

Comments:

-DavidHodge   July 19, 2010
Charles II reigned in 1660-1685. Then James II took over. Andy Murray is Scottish not English. David

DAY 24: GLADESTRY TO KINGTON
THURSDAY, JULY 01, 2010

We had a really short day today because the weather forecast was bad and we were in need of a break.

We walked four miles up and over the hill to Kington and I had one of the most wonderful experiences ever. On top of the hill were more wild horses and this time with fouls. I stood amongst them and felt exhilarated, humbled, honored and comfortably accepted within their herd. I could have remained with them for a very long time.

Kington is a traditional town with a butchers shop, green grocers, ironmongers, newsagents etc and a grocery store not unlike Dr Who's Tardis. If you don't know what a Tardis is, or who, Who is, then never mind but it had a very tiny shop front and a massive interior.

We sat down and had copious cups of tea outside the museum teashop and decided upon a B&B for the night.

B&Bs are all so different making a choice sometimes difficult and they all have their pros and cons. Pubs obviously offer the pub downstairs and therefore the promise of delicious meals and beers right on the premises. There are small hotels, more likely to have baths rather than showers and wifi but aren't at all personalized. Then there are the more homely ones, which tend to be the most interesting and usually offer up a very personal touch. This often includes made to order breakfasts, fresh and home grown ingredients and an opportunity to meet some interesting people and even feel like you are part of the family. Sometimes this can be a little too personal and it makes you wonder how landlords deal with constantly having complete strangers in their living room. Of course, we are nice strangers, but what if we were a couple of sadomasochistic baby killers?

Talked to Curt tonight and he confirmed he is flying out tomorrow with Ivan (who has agreed to leave his friends and the mall for no longer than 2 weeks). Cannot wait to see them.

-posted by Ali using BlogPress from my iPad at 11:01AM

DAYS 25 THROUGH 27: KINGTON TO MONTGOMERY
FRIDAY, JULY 02, 2010 TO SUNDAY, JULY 04, 2010

I have got really behind on the blogging front. It is easy to blog when I am on my own but so much harder once I get company.

This will just be a synopsis of these 3 days so I can get up to date.

Day 25 took us to Knighton or the "Town on the Dyke" in Welsh. We stayed in a converted barn in Knighton behind the George and Dragon pub, which I can highly recommend.

I can visualize Mick now, on top of the Dyke –an earthen mound of approximately 2 feet at this point- brandishing his walking stick and exclaiming in the most proper English accent "Get down you Welsh. Get down and out of my Kingdom". Day 26 we walked to Newcastle; The village of Newcastle in Shropshire (back in England again) obviously, and not the city. We camped at the Clun Valley camping which is not mentioned anywhere in the Dyke accommodation guides but worthy of a mention as it was excellent value at only four pounds per person.

Day 27 we walked through fields of wheat, corn and poppies to reach Montgomery, a gorgeous, quiet and unassuming Welsh border town; with a church, cobble stoned market square, clock tower, ruined castle up on the hill and a fantastic organic café with the most delicious carrot cake I have ever tasted. That evening in the 'magic hour', with the sky full of soft, puffy cumulus clouds and the fading light of a beautiful day, we walked up to the castle and surveyed the 360 degree view of the surrounding countryside and agreed that this was indeed a perfect location for a castle.

-posted by Ali using BlogPress from my iPad at 11:21AM

Dreamy Black Hills and wild horses

A moment of rest

Walking along King Offa's Dyke

'Castle Kitchen' in Montgomery serves the best carrot cake EVER

6

FAMILY

SOMEWHERE OVER THE RAINBOW
TUESDAY, JULY 06, 2010

If I could put music to this particular blog, it would most definitely be Iz Kamakawiwo'ole, singing his beautiful rendition of Somewhere Over The Rainbow.

This blog isn't about walking, England, food or the current state of my feet. It is about my parents and three very devoted sisters paying their final respects; And another reason for my journey here this summer.

This part of my journey begins in North Wales at a family reunion. Curt and Ivan had met up with me in Montgomery – that perfect little border town in my last blog with the brill carrot cake. They had spent three stressful days getting to me via numerous international locations on our now, not so wonderful buddy passes. They were traveling in style with a hire car and it felt kind of bizarre to throw my pack in the boot (trunk) and whiz north, covering miles of Wales in a matter of minutes. Sounds weird to think that in only four weeks I could become so unaccustomed to traveling in a car but these four weeks have been intense and do not equate to time in my normal life.

We dropped Mick back at this home in North Wales (Llandudno) and drove to Capel Curig to be reunited with an extended family that I barely knew existed. Jane and Val are my Dad's sister's children and therefore my cousins. I met up with Jane last year at Dad's funeral but before then I had not seen her for 40 years! It felt as though Dad's death had left Lesley, Jill and I alone but now I stood together with my husband, son, sisters, nephews, nieces, cousins and their extended families, shaking hands, introducing, hugging and I felt far from alone.

We spent hours reminiscing, trying to piece together fragmented memories, looking at old photographs, speculating on why we had drifted so far apart and wishing so much, that we had done this while Dad was still alive.

But now it was time to put mum and dad to rest. We had decided it should be on Tryfan, a mountain that stood out in our child hood memories as a family favourite.

Dad had been keeping mum in a shoebox since her death seven years ago, a box that I had unknowingly almost thrown away. Dad had reassured me then, that he couldn't bear to part with her and wanted to be reunited with her ashes upon his death. Dad was now in a plastic bag and it was time to make that reunion happen so they could rest together in a more appropriate place than a plastic bag and shoebox.

As the three of us drove down Llanberris pass towards Tryfan we were faced with a view that never fails to take my breath away. A view so imprinted in my memory from so many happy childhood walking trips. Tryfan stands bleak and imposing, a landscape of grey rocks, green mosses and soft purple heathers. Waterfalls, static and white from a distance, tumble and flow down the mountainside. On top, clearly visible this morning stand Adam and Eve, two massive Stonehenge type rocks. It is customary to jump between these rocks, suffering exposure and even death from the sheer drop to one side but gaining the 'Freedom of Tryfan' in doing so.

Perhaps a little apprehensively we started up the 'Heather Terrace' and the path that we always took with mum and dad. With impeccable timing, as if ordered as a tribute, two spitfires came roaring low overhead, twisting and turning down the narrow valley.

I carried mum on my back. Jill carried Dad. Lesley carried the sandwiches.

As we walked we remembered:

"Do you remember the picture you had taken over there, Jill? You had just had your haircut and your jeans were all rolled up and I thought you looked really cool. That picture of you with pigtails, Lesley, I think it was taken there. Jill, do you remember when you had to rescue me? I must have been about five; I was eating Bovril crisps and fell off the side of the mountain. You pulled me to safety and I never dropped a crisp, so mum used to say............"

The same paths, the same walls, stiles and rocks that were here 35 years ago; We had changed so much over the ensuing years, but yet this landscape remained the same. Tryfan would never change, sealing in those memories forever and making it a perfect place to leave mum and dad.

We scrambled on up to the top and ate lunch, delaying our task for a little longer. It felt oddly comforting to have them on our backs and sad that we would be going back down without them.

It was very windy and cold and we could delay no further.

We opened up the containers and their ashes flew out and joined together in the wind. It was a magnificent, beautiful experience, exhilarating and happy and not at all sad as we had expected. We were laughing as they blew into the distance or fell at our feet. The two solitary rocks, Adam and Eve looked on, knowing that they would not be jumped by us; as today, the freedom of Tryfan belonged to Brenda and Tony.

As we turned to leave the summit and started the climb back down, we could almost hear a soft Yorkshire accent whispering through the wind ...."Ah well dun lasses".

Now, when I think of mum and dad, I imagine them kissing in the wind, as they blow over the mountains and valleys of North Wales and settle together forever, to form new rocks and life upon Tryfan.

"Somewhere over the rainbow, way up high,
And a dream that you dreamed of Once in a lullaby"

-posted by Ali using BlogPress from my iPad at 11:55AM

Comments:
-sarah   July 20, 2010
sO perfect
-LLWright   July 23, 2010
What an amazing story. Thank you so much for sharing it. I had a similar feeling when I put Dennis in the Colorado River
-Linda   July 25, 2010
Ah, Ali. Was lovely, truly so, to be part of your account of putting dear Tony and his wife Benda to rest. I am thinking that anyone

reading this account feels the love your family was fortunate to share. I shed a tear then came out of it with a smile and continued on with the read to catch up on your tales.

Tryfan

Reminiscing about our childhood walks

Bye mom and dad. RIP together at last.

"It was a magnificent, beautiful experience, exhilarating and happy and not at all sad......"

Sisters return hand in hand

"Somewhere over the rainbow"

7

OFFA'S DYKE – PART 2

DAY 28: WELSHPOOL TO FOUR CORNERS
FRIDAY, JULY 09, 2010

I assume by now you have figured out that I am only numbering the walking days. No sure why I am doing it this way but for the sake of continuity, I will continue to do so.

We actually spent a couple of days in Capel Curig in self- catering accommodation pre-booked by Jill many months ago. It was wonderful to spend time with my family and get to know my cousins after all these years. We vowed this was the first of many reunions.

Curt then drove us back to Mick's in Llandudno, we left the rental car there and took a train back to Welshpool to pick up the Offa's Dyke trail about ten miles north of Montgomery.

It was now time to walk with Curt and Ivan and it was so wonderful to finally have them with me. I desperately wanted them to understand and feel all that I was experiencing.

From the train station at Welshpool we quickly found the footpath to rejoin the Offa's Dyke trail.

I was proudly sporting a new backpack with a few necessary additions, such a pockets and a hydration bag. Ivan was now using my backpack and a pair of my old boots that he swore fit him. He walked on down the towpath of the canal kicking his football (earlier, in an effort to persuade him to come, I had suggested he kick the football along LEJOG and perhaps make the Guinness Book of Records – no go!) but within minutes the boots were killing him. He changed into his boat shoes and then eventually walked the next five miles in bare feet. He gave up on the football thing not long after that.

We left the canal and followed the trail along the Severn River. It was here amongst the fields of cows that Ivan decided he needed shoes. Curt had fortunately brought a spare pair, which Ivan ended up wearing for the rest of the walking. Three sizes too big, but better Ivan thought than having cow poop squelch between his toes.

Speaking of cows, Ivan just loves them. I don't think these cows had ever experienced an 'Ivan' before, with head and unruly hair wrapped in a Rasta head scarf, Tartan boxers proudly showing above his sagging cut-off jeans, loud purple T shirt, sleeves rolled up to reveal manly biceps and of course the oversized shoes. They looked curiously out the corners of their eyes and kept a cautious distance as Ivan tenaciously attempted to feed them with tufts of grass. [Ivan gets his love of animals from both Curt and I – hence the reasons for our vegetarianism]

It was an easy flat day of walking today and we arrived at the B&B ten miles later, still relatively happy.

This was a very posh B&B, in a big Georgian house with an equestrian centre, fussy dead animals for blankets and bathrobes for use after a dip in the deluxe corner tub. Not really a typical English B&B for my boys to experience but fun never the less. We joined another fellow boarder for the evening and got a cab together to the local pub for dinner and drinks.

A successful day by all accounts; Ivan is happy and seems to be enjoying himself despite the fact he cannot understand why we would want to walk all day long for fun.

-posted by Ali using BlogPress from my iPad at 12:31 PM

Comments:

-LLwright   July 23, 2010

OMG Ivan is so big and handsome!

DAY 29: FOUR CORNERS TO SELATTYN
SATURDAY, JULY 10, 2010

So we had a discussion over breakfast time about this business of walking for fun.

We explained to Ivan that fun has a different connotation for us parents. In fact fun, is not how I would describe walking anyway.

Pleasurable is perhaps a better word. Pleasurable because I am simply outside walking and therefore not doing something less pleasurable – paying bills, cleaning, organizing etc – but definitely 'Fun' when I stop and finally sit down in an amazing pub with a beer. In fact, that's it, that IS what it's all about and something I cannot expect a fourteen year old to understand. It has taken me forty-three years to discover that the ingredient to happiness (my happiness anyway) lies in contrasts. I think that in order for me to appreciate the mundane nature and comfortableness of every day life, I have to mix it up. Because after all, how can one appreciate not suffering if one has never suffered? The irony it seems, is that we spend all of our lives trying to achieve a certain level of comfort and do not realise that we may need a little discomfort again to appreciate it.

Not to mention the tremendous physical benefits of walking.

We made the mistake today of thinking this would be a short day. We lingered over breakfast and didn't leave until nearly 11 a.m.. For some reason, without checking the map, I thought we only had about an eight-mile day.

Offa's Dyke decided to zigzag it's way inefficiently all over England and Wales today. We spent miles walking around a canal, which was stunningly beautiful, but the road would have got us to the same place within minutes.

We lunched on top of a hill, thinking we had traveled miles but the village we had departed from hours ago was still clearly visible and disappointingly close.

I am usually very intuitive when it comes to mileage and time of day but on this day all that ability left me. We had obviously entered into a weird time and space warp.

Ivan was questioning our sanity more than ever, but his sense of humor and obvious physical fitness never failed him and he walked admirably on.

We walked for nine hours and finally arrived, tired and desperate at our destination, The Cross Keys pub in Selattyn (back in England again).

This pub doesn't serve food and doesn't have accommodation but was chosen because it was in Mick's 2005 pub guide. It does have great beers. It is also 17th century, beautiful and traditional. We had called in advance and they had agreed to let us camp on their lawn.

I had told Phil and Hilda the hospitable publicans (only the third owners since 1900) that we would be arriving about 2 PM but because of this time warp we arrived about 8 PM. We basically fell through the door into the small bar and everyone was instantly aware that we had arrived.

It was also blatantly obvious (thanks to Ivan) to all at the pub that we had not had any dinner and had no prospects of any.

One of the locals suggested he run us down to the local Chinese/chippie a few miles away. Ivan thought that was a grand idea and made lots of satisfied noises as he inhaled his egg fired rice and veggie chow mein – which he more than deserved.

-posted by Ali using BlogPress from my iPad at 01:19 PM

DAY 30: SELATTYN TO LLANGOLLEN
SUNDAY, JULY 11, 2010

We set off earlier today:

1.Because we weren't in a comfortable bed and breakfast but instead camped under an apple tree and sleeping atop a bed of fallen apples.

2. Because we were psyching ourselves up for a really long day to avoid the mistakes of yesterday.

It was somewhat sunny with a cool breeze, so perfect walking weather and time seemed to be back to normal again.

We made good time and the turrets of Chirk castle quickly came into view above the trees of the green and lush Ceirog valley

Down the valley and then up by the castle to find the national trust farm shop open for business. Lucky for us, because most things seem to be closed on Sundays and Ivan was tremendously happy as he had not partaken in the Chinese left over breakfast. Tea and Bakewell tarts - yummy.

At Froncycylite we had chips and curry sauce before walking over the impressive Pontcysyllte Aqueduct that carries the LLangollen Canal over the river Dee. This aqueduct, built by Thomas Telford, is the longest and highest in Britain and canal boats cruise lazily over the bridge in a cast iron trough, suspended 126 feet over the river Dee supported by masonry arches and piers. I found it quite scary to walk over, reminding me of my irrational fear of heights. Once over, I wanted to stop for another treat - not satisfied with Chinese, Bakewell tarts and chips with curry sauce - but the boys wanted to get the next five miles over with and get settled in LLangollen.

By the way in order to pronounce Llangollen correctly you have to start by forming your lips and tongue to pronounce the L, but instead just blow air gently around the sides of the tongue and that is the "Ll".

Try reading the next paragraph out loud. It is English but written using the sounds of the Welsh alphabet:

"Ai hop ddad yw can ryd ddys and ddat yt meids sens tw yw. Iffy w can ryd ddys, dden yw sawnd ryt and ar redi tw gow hycing in sals. Gwd Inws and Haf ffyn."

It seemed like a very long way along the tow path of the canal to Llangollen and we ended up getting a cab to the hotel as it was a couple of miles out of town.

Spain won the world cup tonight.

Llangollen ended up being the end of Offa's Dyke trail for me, 35 miles short of the end in Prestatyn. Curt and Ivan needed to get back to Mick's to pick up their rental car and drive to Gatwick airport to fly home ☹

I will miss them.

-posted by Ali using BlogPress from my iPad at 02:50 PM

Comments:

-LLWright   July 26, 2010

Thanks for the Welsh tutorial. I have a basic grasp because of studying ancient Welsh harp music, but that really helps! Interestingly, that same LL sound is made in Navajo.

So cool the boys got to come and experience part of your journey chapter

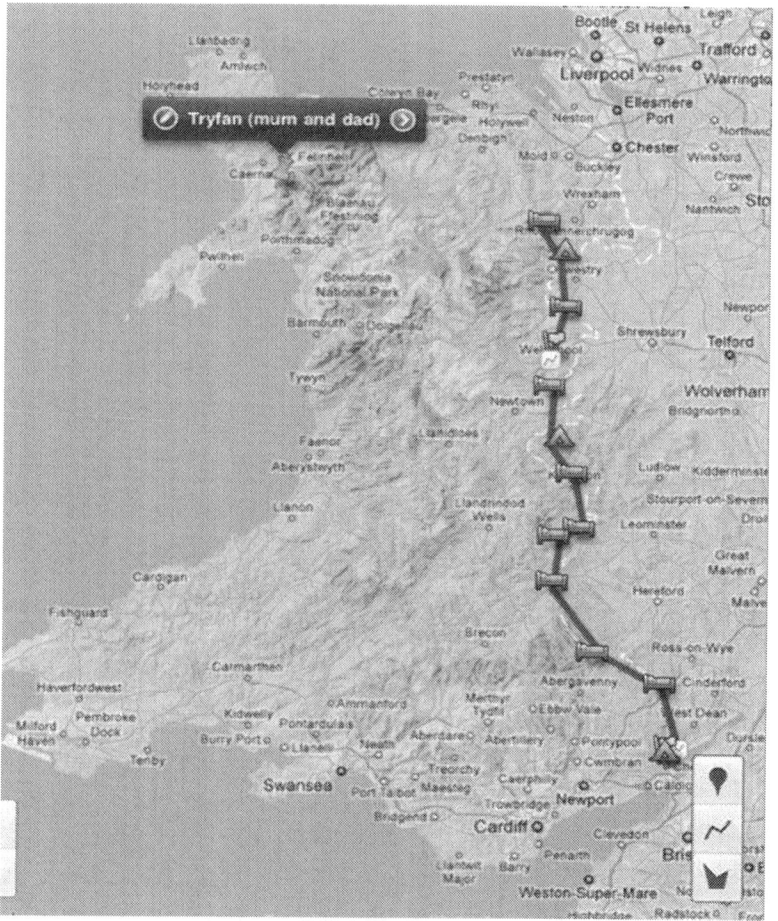

Offa's Dyke

My boys join me to walk Offa's Dyke part 2

The morning after.

The bad boys of Offa's Dyke

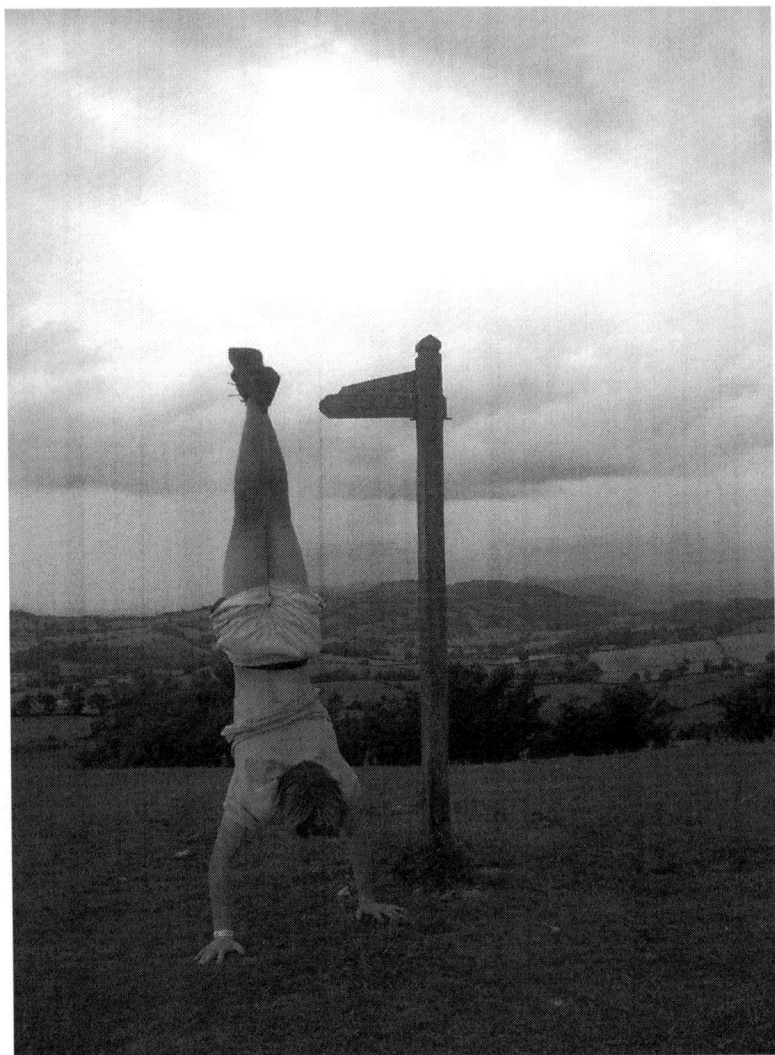

Ivan decides its easier to walk on his hands

Crossing the Pontcysyllte viaduct

Llangollen

8

PENNINE WAY

DAY 31: START OF THE PENNINE WAY
FRIDAY, JULY 16, 2010

It felt like a momentous occasion to be standing at the Nags head pub and the official start of the Pennine Way.

Curt and Ivan left yesterday for Gatwick airport and Mick dropped me in Edale to begin the Pennine Way. I am back on my own for a while and it feels both exciting and a little scary.

But I am now equipped with the entire set of maps for the trail and a compass.

And I am ready for my biggest challenge yet – THE Pennine Way.

This trail starts in the Peak District national Park and travels due north over the South Pennines, through Yorkshire Dales national Park, the bleak and remote North Pennines, traverses Hadrians wall, through Northumberland National Park and the Cheviot hills before entering into Scotland where it ends at Kirk Yetholm. Two hundred and seventy miles in total and is considered the toughest of all the national trails.

To date (July 16th) I have walked for 31 days and have covered 335 miles (353 including today). Let me just state that my feet have walked all that way. Not bad for a cripple that usually has hard time getting out of bed in the morning.

I set off from Edale with iPod on and happily marched along the trail with head down. After passing through several gates, I suddenly realized that I hadn't noticed an acorn (the official national trail symbol) for a while. Chastising myself and realizing that I needed to take more care with route finding, I got out the guide book (yes I have a guide book AND maps) – that's when Sarah came wandering by, another lone female walking the Pennine Way.

Meeting up with Sarah at that spot was in hindsight very fortunate for me. Mick had tried to explain how severe this trail can be, both in terrain and weather but I did not have a concept of this until I was there and experiencing it for myself.

About half and hour out of Edale it began to rain and as we climbed towards Kinder Low the wind began to howl and the mist descended. We could only see a couple of feet in front of us and the path petered out onto a confusing plateau of grit stone rocks and peat bog. There were no acorn signs to direct us up here and without a compass we would surely have been doomed.

Somewhere along here we met up with another couple that were in the throws of a tiff as to which way to go. Heather, as I was later to find out her name, kept on saying how thankful she was to have met up with us, as her husband, "bless his heart", was "useless and bound to get us lost". I must have looked the part, wafting my compass into the mist but I did admit to her that I had only a five-minute instruction the night before on how to use the thing. She was happy to tag along anyway and although looking a little dejected, I think hubby was glad too.

But man, am I glad Mick gave me that lesson because it was invaluable and we were able together to navigate through the mist.

After sixteen miles of viewless, misty moorlands, I said goodbye to my new comrades as they were staying in a B&B and I was walking onto the youth hostel a couple of miles away. We had made brilliant time because we had not stopped once. I had marched for eight straight hours with water pouring down my neck and my feet squelching in my boots. I was ready to stop and get dry.

I am now at the Crowden youth hostel and in a bit of a mess. I can barely walk and took the elevator labeled 'disabled only' up to my room. I am not sure of my ability to walk to the dining room for breakfast tomorrow, let alone miles on the Pennine way.
-posted by Ali using BlogPress from my iPad at 03:24 PM

DAY 32: CROWDEN TO DIGGLE
SATURDAY, JULY 17, 2010

Thankfully my feet were a little better when I awoke and I was able to get to breakfast without using the elevator!

I had only made vague plans to meet up with my friends again but as I hobbled up to where the trail started, there they were, with amazing timing. At the same time it started to rain again.

On with the waterproofs that aren't waterproof at all.

FYI – I am wearing all Patagonia stuff, their Gortex® equivalent. It looks good but seems to be utter crap functionally. Love Patagonia otherwise.

Lessons learnt from yesterday were to follow the map, set compass bearings and know where I am at all times, even when on a well-defined trail. You never know when the trail will disappear or when the mist will descend.

I know, I know......I have scoffed at this in the past but it is essential here and now I am actually finding it fun to map read.

So I strode (hobble fading) out in front of my posse (Sarah, Heather and Martin) leading the way up the misty valley. Yesterday had taken me by surprise but I knew what to expect today. I was already starting to understand this trail.

We initially had a view but that quickly changed and it was more of yesterday; bleak, baron and isolated moorland with driving rain, howling winds and yes...mist.

It was quite amusing to meet fellow hikers (not many of them mind you) walking the opposite direction. They would appear suddenly out of the mist, a couple of feet in front of me, water pouring forwards off their hoods, noses and chins, flowing backwards over and down their fluorescent back pack covers to meet the mud streaking up their legs, mumbling a nonchalant "Good morning" as they battled side ways against the wind to pass me.

Martin was a little grumpy and questioning quite rightly why he was doing this. His wife reminded him it was because he loved her and she wanted to do it.

Although some views would have been nice, I was still enjoying the experience of it all. For me the weather is part and parcel of the experience and synonymous with the moors. Anything else would not have been right.

And then we arrived at Snoopy's snack van - Martin was then happy too.

Two rounds of tea for all of us and a cake for me. The rain also conveniently stopped for us to enjoy this treat.

'Everyone' was at the snack shack. You get to know fairly quickly who is walking the trail with you as you meet up with them sporadically, at various stopping points. As far as I can tell there is only Sarah and I, three Yorkshire lads with their dog and a solo guy, doing the entire trail and on my schedule - so to speak (Martin and Heather are doing a two day package deal and are done today). It was like we were old buddies as we delighted over our hot mugs of tea and discussed our destination points.

But there are consequences to all actions and the tea made for frequent future pee stops - incredibly awkward when walking in a crowd, with a backpack, in rain etc.

And 'Solo' guy had eaten a greasy cheeseburger which he complained bitterly about as we stormed past him on the trail.

At the road to Diggle, Sarah and I turned left and Martin and Heather turned right to get picked up and taken back to their B&B. They were done.

I had called ahead and reserved a spot in the same B&B as Sarah because actually, this was the only place available. The weather that had lifted somewhat, came back in vengeance and we arrived soaking wet.

-posted by Ali using BlogPress from my iPad at 04:37 PM

DAY 33: DIGGLE TO BADGER FIELDS FARM (HEBDEN BRIDGE)
SUNDAY, JULY 18, 2010

Good news is I am staying in a fantastic B&B at Badger Fields Farm, just north of Hebden Bridge.

Bad news is both my camera and iPod have stopped working. Despite being in a plastic bag, in the pocket of my 'waterproof' jacket, they must have got too wet. Therefore there are no pictures of today and won't be anymore until I can buy a new camera ☹

The B&B in Diggle was nothing to rave about. It belongs to a very sweet and very deaf, elderly couple who had the TV turned up to unimaginable volumes and then had to shout (in terrific Yorkshire accents) at each other to be heard. About 10 pm, I heard Sarah go downstairs and very politely ask them to turn the TV down. The bed wasn't great either, with enormous springs sticking up in multiple locations and compared poorly to my Thermarest. But they made good poached eggs and I like the name of their village, Diggle.

It was also odd because our elderly landlady kept on commenting on the weather and how warm it was and failed to note that it was bucketing down with rain and blowing a gale. We kept on hinting about a ride up the road until I finally came out and asked them. They kindly obliged for a small fee.

It was a long steep road to rejoin the Pennine way so we were very glad of the lift.

I spent another day walking in the good company of Sarah. She used to be a lawyer but has just recently been ordained into the Church of England. Come September she begins her career as Curate in a parish and will then be tied for years to come. Sounds very scary to me but I wish her all the best and admire her for following her 'calling'.

Today the Pennine way took us across the M62 motorway and I found it quite thrilling to cross the pedestrian bridge with the roar of traffic and civilization below. It was such a startling juxtaposition to the moorlands and our life on the path.

We walked on, across more desolate moorlands accompanied by the usual squall and deluge, to the high point at Blackstone Edge and then down to the A58, crossing our fingers that the White House Pub would be open.

Amazingly it was open and was serving up food. After we had settled in with sandwiches, soup and plenty of hot tea, our three Yorkshire lads with the dogs showed up and we compared notes yet again. I rung up Badger Farms and booked myself in, as I was definitely not camping in this weather.

Pubs are wonderful places and it easy to understand why they have survived through the centuries and are so ingrained in the British culture; Always an island of comfort, an oasis of dryness and warmth and as predictable as the atrocious weather. Walking only short distances across the moors brings on an indescribable yearning for a pub.

Miles totaled about 17 today. I seem to be capable of longer distances now. It hasn't got any easier, it still hurts but I suppose I can hurt for longer now!

Badger Farm is lovely and comes highly recommended for Pennine Wayfarers. Very homely and the landlady obviously takes pride in what she does. We were greeting with a big pot of tea and chocolate cake. Dinner was incredible with tasty homegrown veggies, potatoes mashed and roasted, a delicious home made cheese flan, all washed down with a glass of red wine. We even had a pudding of chocolate brownie and ice cream.

A quick update on Curt and Ivan as I have just received word from them. They couldn't get a flight out of Gatwick, so they rented another car and drove back to Jill's. They then drove to Birmingham and took a flight to Dublin, Ireland believing they may get a flight home there; but no luck. They ended up having to buy full price tickets back to Salk Lake and scrapped the buddy passes.

What a palaver! Lesson learnt. No buddy passes in the summer.
-posted by Ali using BlogPress from my iPad at 02:34 PM

Comments:
-Sarah Langridge   July 20, 2010
We got right on in Chicago with our buddy passes. Might be a different story going back from Paris though

DAY 34: BADGER FIELDS FARM TO HAWORTH
MONDAY, JULY 19, 2010

My camera appears to be slowly coming back to life. It switches itself on and off, extending and retracting the lens as though it is trying to remember how it used to work. Perhaps there is hope for it yet?

I am currently staying in the 'Secret Garden' room in the Old Registry Guest House in Haworth. I am lounging on the day bed in my en-suite room sipping on a glass of wine and madly posting all the blogs I have been saving up due to lack of Wifi.

I departed from the usual way of the path today and will now be out of synch with all my Pennine chums. It was all getting too chummy really and I want some time on my own to walk alone again. I also wanted to visit Haworth as the Bronte sisters grew up here in the parsonage and wrote their Classics. I am in the heart of Bronte country.

The weather was decent today and when the sun came out it was actually scorching hot by UK standards; truly wonderful to be back in shorts and T-shirt again, to be dry (body and clothes steaming in the warmth) and to see the views of this magnificent landscape. It is a completely different experience to be walking this path without the rain.

Sarah and I walked over Wadsworth moor and up to Within

Heights. At Top Withins stood the ruins of a farmhouse thought to be in Emily Bronte's novel, Wuthering Heights and here, we again met up with the three Yorkshire lads and their dog.

After descending to Ponden reservoir I said goodbye to Sarah and hoped we might meet up again further North.

I hitched a ride into Haworth, which is extremely quaint with beautiful shops and cobbled stone streets, perfect for exploring but....my chaise lounge is awfully comfortable. Besides my boots and socks are wet and the parsonage museum is probably already closed.

Settled, I shall stay in my secret garden room and order up another glass of wine.

Too hard to sightsee AND walk the Pennine Way. Exploration of Haworth can wait.

There goes my camera again. Zip, ziip....

-posted by Ali using BlogPress from my iPad at 03:43 PM

DAY 35: HAWORTH TO ESLACK
TUESDAY, JULY 20, 2010

I must admit to feeling nervous over breakfast this morning, about leaving the security of my deluxe secret garden room and stepping out into the unknown again.

It seems a while since I have truly been on my own. This is a tough environment too and the forecast was for rain all day.

I got a cab back to the reservoir where I had left the Pennine Way yesterday. But first I left my walking stick in the B&B and we had to turn around to retrieve it.

I set out, up through the sodden fields, closely following the guide book directions and map which I had sealed away in plastic bags. I had stuffed my convalescing camera, iPod and phone down in my pack to protect from the weather but that of course made them unusable.

It was only lightly drizzling so it wasn't too bad but it became increasingly misty as I climbed higher onto the moors and I constantly referred to both my map and guide not wanting to get lost.

In one field with a couple of options for paths, I stopped to study the map. Deep in thought and studying it at every angle possible, I felt a gentle nibble on my fingers. The nibble belonged to the wonderfully soft and fuzzy mouth of a particularly friendly sheep and I could feel her teeth as she continued to gently nibble and muzzle me.

All the other sheep in the field had characteristically bounded off at first sight of me but this sheep kept at my side as I walked on, as if guiding me. As I closed the gate on the other side of the field, I thanked her and we said our goodbyes. We looked in each other's eyes and....

Well let's just say, that I think I now believe in reincarnation; so glad that I am a vegetarian. One never knows exactly who or what they may be eating.

I climbed up to Bare Hill, which was indeed bare. Mist.

But as I walked on across the moors the clouds began to lift and a view of Cowling and the beautiful countryside emerged.

I didn't see anyone else on the trail today except for a trail runner who came up rapidly behind, shouted hello and made me literally jump out of my skin.

In Lothesdale the path took me right past the Hare and Hound and not wanting to pass up a refreshment stop, I had a pint of beer and a packet of crisps.

I had been walking without waterproofs as the weather was surprisingly decent but after my snack it all began to change again. As I approached Thornton-on-Craven the heavens opened and the downpour began. Luckily I had a number for a B&B in the area and called for directions. It was however two miles in the other direction so I declined, until she offered to pick me up.

The Grange B&B in Elsack is well worth a stay and they have looked after me very well here. It is a beautiful, almost stately home. I have a big bar of chocolate in my room, a lovely claw foot tub in which to soak, wifi for blogging and all at a very affordable price. Sally has provided me with a bowl of rice for my iPod, as I have been advised that this may serve to draw out the dampness (although, at this point in time, it has been in rice all night and it is still not working), she dried my clothes and even turned on the fire in an attempt to dry out my boots.

-posted by Ali using BlogPress from my iPad at 12:26 PM

DAY 36: ESLACK TO MALHAM
WEDNESDAY, JULY 21, 2010

I am suddenly feeling exhausted. This could be something to do with the pint of beer I have just guzzled at the Lister Arms in Malham and the hundreds of miles I have walked. But I have had the most perfect day.

It was dry and somewhat sunny all day. It all got really superb, when five miles into the walk, I left Gargrave and entered into the Yorkshire Dales National Park and I could see it all spread out in front of me like a flawless patchwork quilt.

I have been in the mist for the last four days but I am sure that the views before me would have been breathtaking under any circumstance and they felt strangely familiar to me. I felt oddly as though I had come home. You see, I am a Yorkshire lass at heart. I was born in Hull, a seaport just south and east of here. Having left Yorkshire at the age of three, I have always considered myself a Londoner but I do feel a deep connection with this countryside.

The scenery around me had definitely changed (not that I have been able to see much for the last few days) and this was unmistakably the Yorkshire Dales. Expansive rolling hills and dales, a jigsaw of various shapes formed by miles of rock walls and a much tamer landscape than the Southern Pennines.

I descended from the hills and the path followed along the scenic banks of the Aire river.

This had to be one of the highlights of my journey so far. Again, it could just be the contrast from walking in the rain and mist but I don't think so as this was incredibly beautiful and bucolic.

The Aire was full and cascaded down between grassy banks, where the odd fly fisherman gracefully cast, whisking rod into the air, back and then forward to land gently on the river. Cows chewed happily in the adjoining fields, beneath large scattered oak trees and it was a tranquil, pleasing scene to walk through. The cows were collared with bells around their necks and shared their fields with horses that wore coats and it seemed as if everything was happy. How could you not be happy if you lived here?

I met a fairly elderly, but amazingly well looking couple and we exchanged stories. They had walked the Pennine Way 40 years ago, at path conception (when it was just a massive quagmire and before flag stones had been placed to span the bogs) and last year completed the entire 630 miles of the South West Coastal path. They also walked from their home in Yorkshire to Rome. They were envious of my exploits and I was in admiration of their devotion to long distance walking and they were an inspiration to me.

It is so exciting and satisfying to catch those first glimpses of your destination and arriving in Malham was no exception. A few rock houses, two pubs, café and YHA nestled in the shadow of Malham

Cove, an impressive curved limestone cliff at the head of the valley with the river Aire running through.

I settled into the YHA and had a shower while I tried to recharge my camera that was now working intermittently but not holding much of a charge.

Once fully charged, I decided to go into the village and ended up walking along a tempting pathway to Janet's Foss. What could this be? The suspense was killing me and the sign said it was only a mile away. I bought an ice cream and ambled along, free of my backpack burden. I was clean, my hair blew freely in the breeze and it felt wonderful to be walking but not to be sweaty and stinky. It was a dreamy path, along a babbling brook, through an enchanted wood, thick with ferns and banks of aromatic wild garlic. The path ended at a beautiful waterfall cascading into a clear pond. The mystery of Janet and her Foss enfolded with an informational board, explaining that Janet is of course a fairy who lives behind the waterfall ('Foss' in Scandinavian).

I made sure I had a drink at both of Malham's pubs and felt really at home in the Buck Inn which advertised itself as a 'Hikers bar. Families, dogs and muddy boots all welcome'.

-posted by Ali using BlogPress from my iPad at 01:37 PM

Comments:

-stromqui   July 21, 2010

I'm still enjoying all of it a heck of a lot. I did not anticipate the excursion to scatter ashes. That was very nice. I'm thrilled with your trip and still really happy for you. Hope you're feeling well

-Anonymous   July 22, 2010

Hi Ali,

I check in with you every morning. Loving it – so proud of you. Pete x

-Mike   July 23, 2010

Great to see all is well – sorry to hear the waterproofs are not – a lightweight poncho could solve the problem!

You'll soon connect with coast to coast trail which follows the same route for a couple of days around Keld – watch out for the Landlord in the old YHA there – he ripped me off overcharging for a bottle of cider!

Mike

Hi Ali,
I have not seen your blog for a while and just checked in. This is so
awesome. Great job girlfriend. Still walking! Wow!

Couldn't get anyone to hike with me in Annecy. Decided I should go
on holiday with you Ali and not my family!!!

DAY 37: MALHAM TO HORTON IN RIBBLESDALE
THURSDAY, JULY 22, 2010

I am sitting in the Pen-y-Ghent café waiting for the bunkroom in
the pub down the road to open. I've already had 4 hot crumpets
drizzled in butter and a gigantic mug of tea. Now I am having a
coffee and waiting for my sister Lesley, to join me. She decided at last
moment to come and be my next walking companion on the trail.

This café is really quite famous and has been open since the
Pennine Way officially opened in 1965. They have volumes of large
books where Pennine Wayfarers have signed in over the years. I
signed my name too and noticed that another chap had also come up
from Lands End, had started a week after me and was in this café
yesterday. So I am not the only nutcase undertaking this kind of
thing.

Lately I have been thinking that the end of the Pennine Way, just
over the Scottish border, may also be the end of my walking for this
summer. From there, it is still a long way through Scotland and I
really don't think I will have enough time to get to John O'Groats.
But now, after seeing that entry in the book, well, I am obliged to
keep going. I can't have that guy get there before me. Not that I am
competitive or anything. My sister-in-law loves to remind me of a
quote I made to her some years ago 'I am not competitive, I just love
to come first'.

Another FYI.....

When I open up my blog now and see the title 'Ali's Mid Life
Crisis', I can't help but think, what crisis? I am definitely not in any
crisis, far from it and don't think I ever have been. I did feel as
though I was at a cross roads in my life and needing to make some
changes both mentally and physically. That, plus my overwhelming
desire to get away from it all and walk for miles and miles must surely
mean I was in the throws of a mid life crisis. And just the inherent

nature of my age – forty something – makes me eligible. It really is an awkward age, not knowing whether to be old or young.

I have successfully walked all my issues away. And my blog now has the wrong title ☺

Today I climbed to the highest point on the Pennine Way at 694m. In fact the path took me over two of the highest peaks in Yorkshire, making it a tough day.

Initially the trail took me right up to the base of Malham Cove, that impressive lime stone cliff I mentioned in my previous blog. Apparently at the end of the ice age a river would have poured over this cliff, forming a mini Niagara Falls, right here in Yorkshire. The trail then ascended steep lime stone steps to get on top of the cliff and I thought for sure that I would hurl my YHA breakfast up.

The trail continued to ascend and took me past the bleak and desolate Malham tarn (old Norse word for pond) and on up to Fountains Fell (old Norse word for mountain). The guidebook says that I was supposed to 'enjoy the magnificent views from here' – NOT. I was in the mist yet again. But it wasn't raining, so all was good.

One thing that has amazed me on this trip is my ability to enjoy my own company. I don't usually you see. I have always needed to be with others to feel comfortable. Well not anymore, because I can walk for hours on my own, not see a soul and love it. The more isolated I am the better.

As I descended down Fountains Fell and out of the mist, my next challenge became visible, Pen-y-Ghent (no, unfortunately not this café and namesake, but a rather large mound en-route to this café). Being one of the highest mountains in Yorkshire isn't claiming much but Pen-y- Ghent was shrouded mysteriously back up in the mist and it could have been as high as Everest for all I knew.

The Pennine Way climbed up its rocky ridge and by the time I had ascended and then descended the other side, I was absolutely shattered. The long walk along the bridle path into Horton on Ribblesdale was painful and endless.

Which is why I am so happy now to be settled in this café.

The pub and bunkhouse eventually opened and I decided to take a shower before Lesley arrived. The following chain of events then caused me a great deal of amusement for the rest of the evening.

I could not get out of the bunkhouse. I tried the door handle every which way, but it appeared to have locked behind me. I was imprisoned, alone, within the walls of a dark and primitive bunkhouse. It smelt of old socks and wet rucksacks with bunk beds and plastic stained mattresses stacked to the ceiling. Earlier I had been glad to find out that Lesley and I were the only ones booked in for the night. Now I wished the bunks were crowded with forty other people. I could be stuck in here for days.

But then I remembered that Lesley was meeting me in the pub and would come to my rescue when I didn't show. So I sat down to wait but then realized I had the pub phone number and more amazingly, I even had a phone signal. So I was rescued and set free, to find that Lesley had just arrived in the pub. This caused us a big giggle as we feasted on our veggie lasagnas.

-posted by Ali using BlogPress from my iPad at 11:17 AM

Comments:

-Trev   August 06, 2010

I'm so glad that your blog has the wrong title, and also glad that you were rescued from the bunkhouse.

DAY 38, HORTON IN RIBBLESDALE TO HAWES
FRIDAY, JULY 23, 2010

Lesley really reminds me of mum because she laughs a lot. Mum would laugh until tears streamed down her face and this must be genetic because actually, all of us Bonner sisters have inherited this trait – especially when together.

We had breakfast back in the Pen-Y-Ghent café and I had more butter with crumpets and another tea in a gallon mug.

Lesley left the café and promptly searched for her car outside, in which to put her lunch. I had to remind her that she was now car-less and gently directed her back to her backpack, the necessary place for her sandwich.

We laughed about this too.

It was fifteen miles to our next destination, Hawes. It was a straightforward track, the weather was warm and sunny and it was not necessary to navigate at all. This made it very easy for us to talk and talk we did, for the entire way.

Lesley is eight years older than me, left for uni and then married before I was old enough to really get to know her. I then left for the USA, she had four kids and we were then too far away, wrapped up in separate lives and too busy. So this was a perfect opportunity to make up for lost time.

She was also joining me on a perfect leg of my journey because we reminded each other that we had in fact spent some time together, many years ago, right here in the Yorkshire Dales. Lesley was nineteen and I would have been eleven and she took me on a road trip to the Dales, after she had just got her drivers license (scary, what were our parents thinking?). Neither of us can remember any useful details however, except that I ate large quantities of white bread and apricot jam, a vague recollection of us being in a chip shop in Hawes and a exasperating multiple point turn on a dead end road. Funny the things we both remembered. What did we actually do for those few days?

Hawes was as beautiful as we kind of remembered it and we had a most civilized B&B pre-booked for the night.

-posted by Ali using BlogPress from my iPad at 11:29 AM

DAY 39: HAWES TO TAN HILL INN
SATURDAY, JULY 24, 2010

The Fairfield B&B was luxuriously civilized in everyway and contrasted so perfectly with our bunkhouse experience the night before.

Moving on and northwards, we left Hawes and set out across the fields, stocking up on bars and lunch items from a whole food shop, aptly named "The Good Life".

We ascended steadily upwards to another high point on the Pennine Way and ate our yummy lunch. This consisted of pita breads, squeezable mushroom pate and Wensleydale cheese. Of course Hawes is in Wensleydale. I cannot say Wensleydale without Wallace and Gromit coming to mind, with visions of large clay hands excitedly shaking, a wide mouth with oversized teeth saying "cheeeeese gromit?" and freshly sheered sheep, stacked atop a motorcycle in a triangular formation, whizzing through the Yorkshire Dales. If you haven't seen Wallace and Gromit, then you must, - brilliantly funny and clever.

This was a long day of walking (17 miles) and we ended it by climbing again across the soggy moors towards Tan Hill Inn.

Tan hill Inn is the highest pub in Great Britain. As we came over the brow of the hill, there it was, situated on top of the desolate moors, shrouded in mist and looking heavenly. I could not hobble fast enough to get in the door and had to step over sheep sheltering in the doorway to get in.

The bleak landscape of its location, its cold grey exterior and quietness of the moors was a complete contrast to within. Inside a coal fire burned and bar was crowded and noisy. The fire and gentle inner lighting warmed the cold flagstone flooring, where dogs wandered between the multitudes of legs, hoping to get scraps. The pub cat unperturbed by all this commotion, lay peacefully sleeping curled up on the piano stool. The atmosphere was buzzing in anticipation of the evening's entertainment, a blue grass band from Nashville.

By midnight Lesley and I were merrily singing along with a particularly raucous rugby club, celebrating a stag night. Then we had to find our tent amongst dozens of others randomly scattered on the misty moors outside.

It had been another brilliant day of contrasts and connections.

-posted by Ali using BlogPress from my iPad at 09:39 AM

Comments:

-trev   August 06, 2010
Oh, doorway sheep!

-LLWright   August 09, 2010
As soon as you said "Wensleydale," I had the exact same imagery come to mind!

DAY 40: TAN HILL INN TO BALDERSDALE
SUNDAY, JULY 25, 2010

Morning on the moors was characteristically brisk, damp and misty, as bodies emerged slowly from their tents, nursing hangovers and hungry for breakfast.

Breakfast at the pub was a lovely shambles. Too many people had been camping, bed and breakfasting or staying at the bunkhouse last night. Too many people for this quirky pub to deal with and everyone just ended up helping themselves to breakfast items in the kitchen.

Lesley was taking a cab to Kirby Stevens railway station and catching a train back to Horton on Ribblesdale to pick up her car, so we had to say goodbye ☹ (but Lesley was excited to be traveling on the Settle to Carlisle railway, supposedly the most beautiful railway line in the country and a favorite of our dad's — fitting in yet again with the greater theme of this story).

I was then on my own again and set off north across the lonely, desolate and boggy moors. The Inn, its security and its inhabitants were soon lost back in the mist. I quickly gave up on keeping my feet dry and focused instead on not getting sucked up to my waist in bog. The flagstones that usually spanned the bogs were noticeably missing on this section of the Pennine way, making navigation tricky. Luckily the mist lifted as I descended in elevation and marker posts became visible at intervals in the distance across the moors. Initially down hill and then fairly flat, I made good time despite an annoying pain in my toes.

Once off the moors, I followed a track for a short distance and a cute little tractor appeared up over the brow of a hill, followed by more cute little tractors. Never really thought of a tractor as cute but these were reminiscent of the ones I would have been proud to own in my childhood Matchbox collection, gaily colored, compact and chugging slowly along. I waved at all the drivers as they passed and they proudly waved back. It was a sight to behold and could possibly explain a sign that had perplexed me a couple of days ago (this particular Pennine way sign also had a plaque of a tractor on it, labeled with coast to coast). The Coast to Coast is another popular national trail that goes across the country east to west and I do believe these tractors may have been following this path. Oh how brilliant and only in England.

My toe pain continued to get worse, so I cut my day short about ten miles later at Clove Farm B&B conveniently located right on the path. They were full but she squeezed me into her daughter's room, brought me tea and cake and me feel very welcome.
-posted by Ali using BlogPress from my iPad at 09:44 AM

BALDERSDALE TO LANGDON BECK
MONDAY, JULY 26, 2010

Had the most freshest, most delicious poached eggs for breakfast.

As I walked I thought about the question posed to me over breakfast by my hosts, "Aren't you scared walking alone?" This has been asked of me several times and I can never come up with anything better than "no". So now I was asking myself why.

I think it's because I am generally a positive person and don't believe that any harm will come to me. I don't think walking is particularly hazardous. I have a long history of walking and never get into any problems so I suppose I am also fairly confident. I could get lost or hurt myself but even then, I feel I would manage and seek help somehow. I feel these are just the normal hazards of life. I am lucky because I don't tend to worry about what could happen. I find enough to worry about, without getting anxious over the never-ending possibilities of what may happen.

Perhaps foolish but I am glad I think this way; otherwise I would not be on this journey.

And anyway, I was about to have another walking companion. Mick had made last minute plans to join me again. I was on my way to meet up with him in Middleton on Teesdale, about seven miles on.

Having always chosen to walk abroad and having completed numerous expeditions to the Himalayas, walking in Britain has never really been on Mick's radar – too tame I suppose.

But now it seems Mick has also been bitten by the long distance walking bug and even here, in Britain.

I really enjoy his company so I am happy to have him along again. Plus he is delivering my weekly shot to me.

One hundred and forty miles into the Pennine way and I am over half way there. Feeling pretty happy about this and my feet, despite feeling bad yesterday seem to have recovered yet again.

Mick found me hunkered down in a tearoom guzzling tea and engrossed in my James Herriot book (courtesy of the last B&B). The Yorkshire Dales is 'James Herriot country' and I always enjoy getting into the spirit of things with a pertinent book.

We walked on together towards Langdon Beck Youth Hostel, another seven miles on but down a gentle river path by Low and High Falls.

-posted by Ali using BlogPress from my iPad at 09:53AM

DAY 42: LANGDON BECK TO DUFTON
TUESDAY, JULY 27, 2010

This has probably been my most favourite day of walking so far.

We left Langdon Beck Youth Hostel with the forecast being all doom and gloom.

And began walking up the remote river valley to follow the River Tees. Through meadows, fields and bogs, over stiles and boulders until we reached the impressive Cauldron Snout. Aptly named, the river boils furiously over a narrow rock gorge and we scrambled up the side, over slippery rocks polished by the many boots of fellow

Pennine Wayfarers.

As the path then ascended over the remote moorlands of the North Pennines and as if mandatory for this landscape, the forecasted mists and rains descended.

It was at this point, huddled under my hood, listening to the constant swish of rain trousers and confined to my own thoughts, that I decided not to eat any more veggie sausages. I am now officially fed up of English breakfasts veggie style. The veggie sausages eaten this morning were now playing havoc on my stomach. Yes tomorrow I would have muesli and may not even have any eggs.

Amazingly, as we arrived on top of High Cup Nick the mist and clouds lifted to reveal the most glorious valley I have ever seen - a U shaped valley with a river snaking its way along the bottom and into the distant mists. The valley sides rose smoothly up in a carpet of green with grey rocky swaths, to an impressive cliff that horseshoed its way around the rim. As the mist lifted further, we could see in the distance the Western mountains of the Lake District and the Vale of Eden spread before us.

The sun came out and the views remained as we began the long descent to the beautiful village of Dufton.

-posted by Ali using BlogPress from my iPad at 10:01AM

DAY 43: DUFTON TO GARRIGILL
WEDNESDAY, JULY 28, 2010

Over breakfast (no veggie sausages) our Landlord, Ray, insisted on presenting us with a terrifying picture of our day ahead.

The guidebook does say this is the longest and toughest day on the Pennine Way and these hills do hold the English records for bad weather. But I do think he went a little overboard and insisted we call him once off the hills and descending. If we didn't call he would send out the mountain search and rescue. Scary. I was more nervous about not having a cell phone signal to make that all-important call.

Did we have good navigational skills? We assured him that we did.

We left the B&B and about 20 yards away, within full view of our concerned Landlord, took a wrong path. We had to back track and nipped quickly around the corner in a hope that he had not seen us. But I feared he was already on the phone to search and rescue, warning them of our pending requirements for rescue.

Once back on the Pennine way we confidently made our way up the long ascent to Great Dun Fell and then across broad sweeping plateaus to Cross Fell (I may have said this before but this is most definitely THE highest point the Pennine Way – 893m).

And of course the weather was atrocious.

Torrential rain and thick clag (northern for mist). Visibility was once more terrible and it became a wonderful exercise in navigation and I really enjoyed putting my newfound compass skills to test. But also glad Mick was with me!

From out of the clag, two shapes in the form of wet Englishmen descended and headed towards us.

It was Mick that initiated the typical English greeting: "A good day for it, isn't it" And the reply: "Yes comes and goes...old chap, what, what"

And they disappeared back into the clag.

Unable to break because of the weather (that hadn't 'gone' at all but had been full on), we were happy to reach Greg's bothy (hut) to stop for a limp cheese sandwich, a YHA left over. Soaking wet from my non water-proofs and freezing cold, I layered on all the dry stuff I could find.

The door of the bothy swung open and in walked 'Mr Dry' as he is known to us now. I couldn't initially figure out why he looked so strange but then it registered. He was bone dry, clean, sporting a pair of binoculars around his neck and looking as though he had been on an afternoon stroll of bird spotting.

How could he have possibly been in the same weather as us? So, unable to curb my curiosity, I asked...

He proudly whispered, as if letting me into a big secret, that he used a small umbrella. Oh, I said as if it explained it all, but could not for the life of me figure out how that had kept him so immaculate and in all that wind and wildness.

Will you be stopping the night here? asked Mr Dry As if we were in a plausible establishment.

I looked around at the cold, wet floors of the primitive rock bothy and could not imagine staying any longer than completely necessary. Spend the night? Was he nuts?

I turned to answer but Mr Dry had mysteriously disappeared.

As we left to once more brave the elements outside of the bothy, we both agreed that had been incredibly strange. Had Mr Dry been an apparition? Could he have been The Greg of Greg's bothy?

It was a massively long ascent in Garrigill on a boring, hard track and we were so looking forward to the pub.

On arrival, the George and Dragon was all boarded up and horribly closed. But oddly enough and as unbelievable as this may sound, in the middle of a small roundabout in the centre of the village was a barrel of beer and hand pump. A couple of the villagers were pulling pints and offering us a glass to join in. More locals began to show at the pump, filled their sundry of containers with free beer and merrily sat on the roundabout in defiance of the closed pub.

Oh and lastly, we did remember that phone call to Ray in Dufton. Can only hope that he receives my message that we got down safely, otherwise search and rescue could be out looking for us now......hic. Love this village!!

-posted by Ali using BlogPress from my iPad at 10:05 AM

Comments

-Trev   August 06, 2010

this is my favorite day yet.

DAY 44: GARRIGILL TO ALSTON
THURSDAY, JULY 29, 2010

Not much to blog about today.

We were treating this as a rest day and only walked 4 miles down a gentle river path to Alston.

Alston is the highest market town in England, although the inhabitants of Buxton that also claims this altitude record dispute this. So they recently measured it and apparently if you measure where the market is, then Buxton wins but Alston ended up with being higher overall so they feel they ultimately won. I suppose every town could claim to have the highest something....the highest toilet, the highest zebra crossing the highest pig pen etc.

Tomorrow I start on the third and final map of the Pennine Way. Ninety miles left on this trail and I am starting to think of the end.

What shall I do next?

I am holding up incredibly well. In fact, holding up is an understatement because I am feeling better that I have done for years. I was starting to feel old before my years, the arthritis making me stiff, tired and constantly achy. All that has gone, my flexibility has returned, my posture improved and I feel young again. I can squat, get myself up off the floor with ease, clench my fists and I am strong and fit. My arthritis appears to be in remission and I am now only suffering in a minor way from the damage it has already caused.

As far as I can tell, I don't seem to be creating any more damage, which is of course the danger of doing this kind of thing.

For doctors that are reading this blog (and I know there are!), I can recommend this prescription for your patients "Take a long walk".

-posted by Ali using BlogPress from my iPad at 10:12 AM

DAY 45: ALSTON TO GREEN HEAD
FRIDAY, JULY 30, 2010

Have been trying to find Internet access to post some of these blogs, but to no avail.

Today was a tough walking day. Seventeen miles of railway track, yet more fields, stiles, moorlands and bogs to end at Hadrian's Wall.

It is becoming apparent that not many people complete this trail.

This could explain why the path towards the end of the day just petered out onto massive moorland devoid of any way marker signs. It was hard to believe we were following a national trail and assumed they couldn't be bothered to signpost it because not enough people made it this far.

We are also starting to hear about dropouts. I forgot to tell you but we met up with the Yorkshire-lads-with-the- dog in the pub the other night. They are now without the dog and without two of their comrades who gave up and went home. Haven't seen Sarah the vicar yet either and it makes me wonder if she has gone home and she said she would, if the weather did not improve. Of course she could be way ahead of me.

Did meet up though with a group of four today going our way. We found it odd that we hadn't met up with them until now but they said they had heard of me. My reputation is preceding me. Made me feel quite special!

We are staying in a bunkhouse tonight next to the ruins on Thirwell Castle. We walk along Hadrian's Wall tomorrow.

-posted by Ali using BlogPress from my iPad at 10:16 AM

DAY 46: GREEN HEAD TO STONEHAUGH
SATURDAY, JULY 31, 2010

Walking along Hadrian's Wall was incredibly tough. Magnificent views of the Northumberland countryside but a roller coaster of steep up and downs.

Hadrian's Wall runs coast to cost where England is at its skinniest. It was built in AD 122 by the Roman Emperor, Hadrian as a fortification to keep the Scottish rabble out of England. The wall is still visible in some places and a remarkable feat of engineering but in others it is completely missing, destroyed over the years to build castles elsewhere.

We were heading for a place on the map called Housesteads, which conjured up images of homely places, such as B&Bs, pubs, eating establishments and of course houses and 'steads'. It was 'In'stead a load of Roman rubble. Once a Roman fort but now just a delightful museum, lacking in hostelries and refreshments.

This caused us to walk a further 6 miles and take a detour slightly off the map to a little village called Stonehaugh.

The moment we left the touristy Wall we were once again in isolation and on boggy moorlands.

We walked the last few miles on forest trails. I became paranoid about map reading and did not fancy getting lost in the maze of spookiness we were walking through. Tall pines lined the path and their tight interior was extremely dark, devoid of any vegetation, weird and very uninviting.

More spookiness was to come as we entered Stonehaugh. This village was unlike any other that I had encountered in my travels. Was I now in Canada? This was not your quaint and typical English village. A forlorn, stark sign marked our entry into Stonehaugh and big logging trucks and shanty type buildings greeted us. All was quiet except for the calling of a strange bird. Spooky, spooky and Mick felt it too. Could this village be full of weirdo's and would we end up in a big pot for dinner? A confused mix of Blair Witch Project and Fargo came to mind.

We arrived at a village green and instantly felt more at home. A row of small gaily-colored terraced houses lined the green on either side and this seemed to be the extent of the village. Although still odd and forgetting the ugly entry into the village, it was actually quite cute. This did not stop us however, fretting over what to expect of the campsite.

To our surprise the campsite was packed with campers and instead of just a basic farmers field, it was civilized with toilets, showers and even a social club. What were all these holiday makers doing in this strange, off the beaten path place?

We headed for the community hall and social club where we had heard they might make us a cheese toasty. The only reason this grand building fit into the village was because it didn't fit and was distinctly odd, like everything else here. No toasties and no food at all that contained any nutritional value. Our dinner consisted of Ales, whiskies, twiglets, scampi fries and fun gums.

But we entertained ourselves with pool and ping pong.

And did find out that this village was purpose built in the 1940s to house the forestry workers. So that fits.....

-posted by Ali using BlogPress from my iPad at 10:23 AM

DAY 47: STONEHAUGH TO BELLINGHAM
SUNDAY, AUGUST 01, 2010

We breakfasted on a cheese and pickle sandwich each, carefully saved from yesterday.

We were walking to Bellingham today. Not in Washington of course and this one is pronounced Bellin'jam.

More forestry trails today. About ten miles and it nearly killed me. Think I may be coming to the end of my abilities. Have I hit my wall? Am I about to find out what happens if I walk too far?

But thankfully Bellinjam contained the most wonderful B&B where I recovered quickly over cheese sandwiches, egg and cress sandwiches, lattes, Mexican spinach balls(?!) and a ploughman platter. In fact the civilized Riverside Hotel, located on a cricket field, contained everything we needed and we didn't even venture into the village to explore. It even had Internet access but the iPad was unable to hook up – hope that it's not screwed up. Really need to post this hoard of blogs.

-posted by Ali using BlogPress from my iPad at 10:28 AM

DAY 48: BELLINGHAM TO BYRNESS
MONDAY, AUGUST 02, 2010

Eggs are magnificent I have decided.

My problem for the last few days has almost certainly been a lack of eggs. Fun gums for dinner and the odd cheese and pickle sandwich for breakfast do not fuel the body enough for this kind of thing. That is obvious Ali....I can hear you thinking this and wagging your finger at me....

After eating a massive wholesome breakfast the Riverside, containing two poached eggs, I found I could walk again. I had a surprising amount of energy and made me realize just how bad yesterday had felt. I need to remember this when I get home and eat eggs way more often.

The guidebook now frequently refers to 'progressive bogginess'. I had thought it boggy before but today was quagmire central.

We had to ascend up a steep bank next to the forest and I felt like I was in the Amazon. I had to fight back the head high greenery, suffer the oppressive humidity, swat the flies and midges, while trying to climb a ninety-degree incline of quag. Two steps up, three slides back and a boot full of thick sludge.

But my eggs were working.

More level bog on top.

A forestry commission sign welcomed us into Kielder Forest with a big 'Welcome Pennine Way Walkers' but a bench to sit on may have been nicer, a fly swatter or some dry ground or even better a cup of tea.

After miles of forest track we arrived in Byrness and stayed at the YHA that had been bought privately by a very enterprising couple. Great to finally find someone dialing into the possibilities of walkers on the national trails.

I spend a lot of time thinking about this as I walk. Thinking about my experiences in the various B&Bs, bunkhouses, campsites and how I would do it differently. It doesn't take much to please us walkers, we are an appreciative bunch but we do have some unusual needs that could easily be accommodated should you know what they are. I won't go into it all now but I know how I would run my accommodation if I had a place on a national trail.

Anyway this couple had it down and were openly proud of themselves.

"We have it all we do here" our Landlord kept on saying as he flung open the various cupboards full of goodies for our purchase and consumption. "Fully licensed we are here" as he showed us his cupboard full of liquor and local ales. "We do bag transport and pick up and drop off. You wash your clothes in this here bucket, spin them in this here machine and hang them here to dry. Breakfast is in the fridge here" as he opened the fridge to reveal individually priced tomatoes, eggs, sausages and slices of bread. "You help yourself and fill out this here slip with how much you owe. 100% occupancy we have here, since we took over."

The last part of our YHA tour took us into an extremely smelly boot room. "You put your boots in this here dry room, fill them with newspaper and put on these here flip flops".

"We have it all, we do here. Dinner will be in an hour"

Too much information and they failed to tell us how to get back in the hostel and Mick and I found ourselves hilariously locked out twice.

Our other concern was how to get more beer from the cupboard, as this one remained locked. "You ring us three times on our mobile and then hang up and we know then that you need more beer and it doesn't cost you the call" he winked "we have everything sorted here".

Brilliant.

And dinner was great. Our Landlady had made mega batches of various dishes and frozen them to be cooked individually. I had veggies and rice in a sweet Thai chili sauce and chocolate sponge with custard for dessert. Yum.

Joining us for dinner was a family from Australia walking John O'Groats to Lands End and doing exactly my route except the other way round. They had been walking for 7 weeks and had been on the Pennine Way three days. And I thought I was so unique. There was also a group of runners we had met previously, doing just a section of the Pennine Way. In fact there was a whole host of people staying here, doing various outdoor activities and for some reason the Youth Hostelling Association had been dumb enough to sell this hostel. Our Landlords had the foresight to realize that they had a captive audience because with only one other B&B in the village, no shop and dare I say it, no pub, where else are we supposed to stay?

The topic of conversation over dinner turned to bog. The next section is again 'progressively boggy' and a story emerged of a guy yesterday going up to his waist in the stuff and had a mucky tidemark to prove it. His cell phone had been ruined and he was incapable of getting out without help. We talked about sucking bogs but were informed that these probably weren't of the sucking kind but they didn't sound too convinced of this.

I will be more careful over the bogs tomorrow.

-posted by Ali using BlogPress from my iPad at 01:59PM

DAY 49: BYRNESS TO HEN HOLE HUT
TUESDAY, AUGUST 03, 2010

We struggled over breakfast with the system. The list on our slip became longer as we gathered breakfast and lunch items together, making it a mathematical nightmare. 15p x 4 butters + 25p x packet of two slices of bread x 4 + 20p per Dairlylee cheese triangle + 20p per Kitkat etc, etc. I think we would have gathered up more food if it hadn't been so mentally exhausting.

Needless to say we left without having enough breakfast or getting enough food to last us through a wild camp tonight. But I did prepare two hard-boiled eggs for the road as I have become psychologically dependent on them.

This was it, our final 29 miles on the Pennine Way, the path goes over the Cheviot Hills and here are no villages, places to stay or refreshments along the way. We were on our own now until the end. And it felt exciting.

I didn't fall in the bog and for the most part they were paved with flagstones or duckboards.

The views were tremendous and the path took us back and forth over the Scottish border. It was wild but tame; windy but calm; cold but muggy; boggy but rugged. All those contrasts that have become so important to me were right there for me to experience all at the same time. I can't tell you how fortunate I felt to be on the last leg of this amazing trail that had taken me up through the heart of a country I adore.

We had planned to camp half way but decided to move on and try and get to Hen Hole Hut.

Twenty-one miles later we arrived exhausted but extremely happy and proud of ourselves to have made it so far in one day. It meant that tomorrow would be a short day and we could be down for lunch, which was good as we had little food left.

Hen Hole Hut was a wooden structure approximately 8x10 feet, sparsely furnished with a bench that ran around the interior, a Visitor book that hung on the wall and a couple of benches outside. Very basic but a welcome shelter from the wild Cheviot weather and it made a good wind block for our tents erected on the leeward side.

Inside the hut we ate our delicious Dairylee and crisp sandwiches. I searched for entries in the Visitor's book of any known people that had come by this way before me. So fun to read all their stories. No sign of any Sarah.

It was windy and cold for an August evening. I layered on all my clothes and snuggled down in my sleeping bag to spend my last night on the Pennine Way.

-posted by Ali using BlogPress from my iPad at 02:07PM

DAY 50: KIRK YETHOLM AND THE END OF THE PENNINE WAY
WEDNESDAY, AUGUST 04, 2010

I ate my last boiled egg and put my tent away.

It was a beautiful view to wake up to and the clouds hung low over the Cheviots. Ahead lay the end of the Pennine Way and spread out in front and below us, the low lands of Scotland.

I could look back and see the route we had taken over hills and along ridges yesterday, it looked a long way and it was amazingly satisfying. I tried to imagine what it would look like if I could see further south, to my entire route. How long would that look? I have walked up and down plenty of mountains in my life but never through and over an entire mountain range. I was proud of my achievement and enjoying how it was making me feel.

We descended down and out of the Pennine range. It was only eight miles today but it was surprisingly hard.

As I placed my last step into the Border Hotel in Kirk Yetholm, I knew it would be my last. Completely psychological I am sure but I felt as though I couldn't walk another step.

Fifty days and six hundred miles later and I was done with walking!

Just as I had done at the beginning of this journey, I had the obligatory picture taken beneath the sign that hung on the wall:

THE BORDER HOTEL
End of the Pennine Way

In the pub I collected and drunk my celebratory free half pint, received my certificate of trail completion and signed the Pennine Wayfarer book.

I did it. I walked the entire Pennine Way.

....

-posted by Ali using BlogPress from my iPad at 02:11 PM

Comments:

-Trev   August 06, 2010

Hooray

-alixnotes   August 06, 2010

Well done!! Alston is my hometown and I came across this blog. I have had a lovely time for the last 30 mins reading your blog.

-Anonymous   August 06, 2010

Congratulations Ali. I am amazed at your achievement and even more amazed at your good health. Like me it seems being happy and unstressed is incredibly beneficial to your physical wellbeing. You heading home now? Love n best wishes Pete x

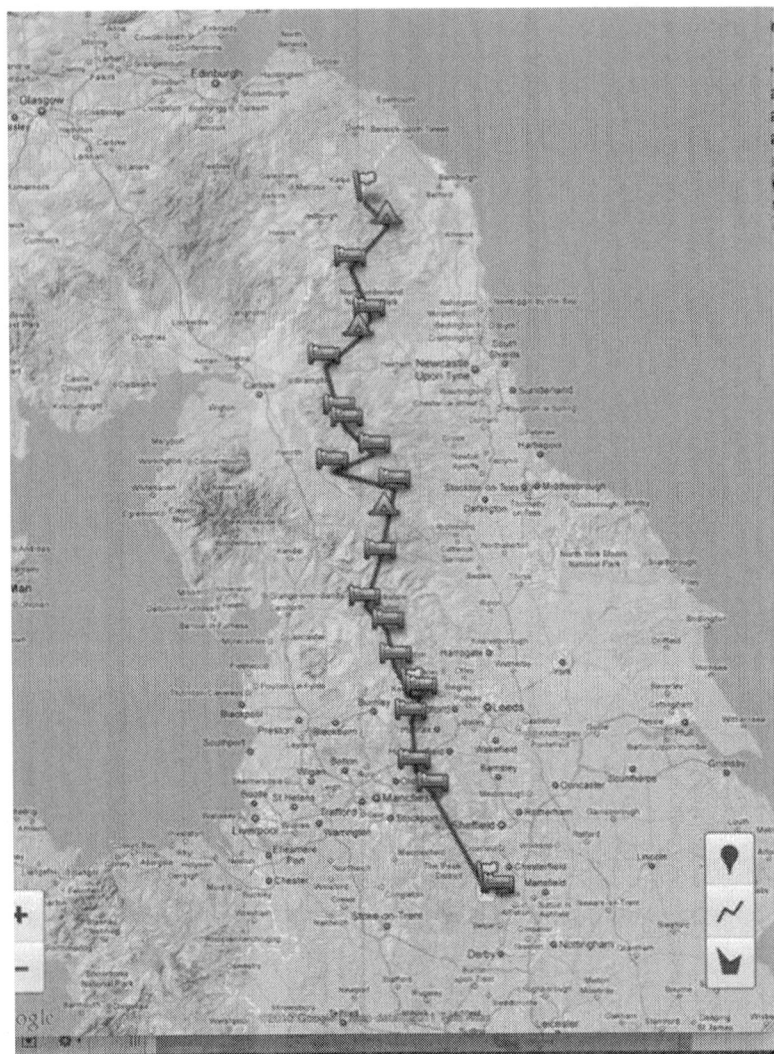

The Pennine Way

The start of the Pennine Way

Snoopy's tea van

The Yorkshire Dales

James Herriot and Wallace and Gromit country

Desolate Malham Tarn

Pen-y-Ghent. Do I have to go over that as well?

Lesley hanging with the doorway sheep at the Tan Hill Inn

Mist lifting over High Cup Nick

The delightful village of Dufton, Cumbria

George and Dragon closed? No worries the roundabout will do.

Hadrians wall and the Northumberland countryside

Descending out of the Cheviots into Scotland.

The end of the Pennine Way – a free celebratory half pint with Mick in the Border Hotel

9

THE END

WHAT TO DO NEXT?
FRIDAY, AUGUST 06, 2010

I am in the Hoot n' Cat coffee shop in Kelso, just over the border in Scotland.

I have this mad idea to buy a bike and continue up to John O'Groats.

I know I am done with the walking but not quite sure that I am done with this adventure. I am waiting for a divine signal to tell me this is the right thing to do. Perhaps I need another latte while I am waiting for this signal?

It's raining, so not particularly inspiring but I can't seem to shake this feeling that I am not done yet.

I've been in the local bike shop and sized up the perfect bike but the rest of the plan is not clear. Lots to consider. How will I get the bike home? What about my backpack? I have to think of my finances too. When should I go 'home'? Will I even be able to get home on my silly buddy pass? More importantly, where am I staying tonight?

Thought it might help to write these questions down but no answers are coming forth yet. Does anyone have any comments on this?

Better order a pot of tea as I may be here in this café for a while longer.

-posted by Ali using BlogPress from my iPad at 05:26 AM

Comments:

<u>-jestfourfun</u>   <u>August 06, 2010</u>
Way to go Ali! Hope there is something left of your feet! Bet you could use a nice cortisone injection.
Sincerely, Dr Rhodes

<u>-Trev</u>   <u>August 07, 2010</u>
Well, you could always take a spot on a sailboat coming to the Caribbean, if you can't get a flight; since you have a tent, I don't think you have to worry too much about where you'll sleep while you're deciding; and you've probably figured everything out by now anyways.

A SUMMER OF ACHIEVEMENTS
SATURDAY, AUGUST 07, 2010

I have decided not to go to John O'Groats. Scotland is a big and beautiful country and not to be hurried through. I shall leave this for another day. Perhaps for a time when I can enjoy it together with Curt.

A bike seems burdensome and after spending so long in isolation on the trails I am not convinced that I want to be riding along side traffic.

John O'Groats was merely a target and gave me a framework and a foundation for this summer. It isn't necessary to get there because my real goals have already been achieved.

I have nothing more to prove to myself at this point in time.

I have reconnected with my place of birth and I have done more than a little walking (as my blog title hoped).

My self-confidence has been revived. I trust my decision- making and know that I am worthy.

My health is superb and no longer in doubt.

I know what makes me happy and feeds my soul. I know I require contrasts in my life and to follow my dreams.

I have accepted that everything physical about my parents and my life with them is now gone. But memories remain and their legacy lives on within my sister and I.

I now have a new relationship with Britain, founded on my childhood but reshaped by my newer experiences. I know my love for this country is real and deep and that I do want to return as soon as possible, to live here and I have ideas on how that could work.

Can you believe I have achieved so much just by walking for two months? This summer has been all I could ever ask for.

My new goal will be to maintain this happiness and newfound fitness and to carry it over into my 'real life'

I want to get back to my husband and son.

-posted by Ali using BlogPress from my iPad at 02:35 PM

WHAT A BEAUTIFUL WORLD
SATURDAY, AUGUST 07, 2010

I want to leave you with a speech that my Dad wrote for his eightieth birthday party. He did not end up delivering this speech, choosing instead a much shorter off the cuff version, so I was delighted to find it last summer in his desk drawer. This party (held in his beloved London home, surrounded by family and friends) in a sense became my father's living wake - he suffered a fatal stroke just before his 81st birthday.

My friends,

It has been a good 80 years

With, what seems to me perfect timing, I have twice this week heard Louis Armstrong singing that evocative song "What a Wonderful World".
Nothing could more aptly express my feeling at this moment

> *"I see trees of green, red roses too*
> *I see them bloom for me and you*
> *I see skies of blue and clouds of white*
> *The bright blessed day, the dark sacred night*
> *And I think to myself what a wonderful world"*

And it is to you my friends that have made it so.

My neighbours-my colleagues in the Liberal Democrats- above all-my family.

I am often asked if it isn't about time I downsized and got rid of this house, which is far too big for me. But I love this house. Brenda and I must have been shown round more that 50 houses when we moved down here from Yorkshire. I have lived here now for more than half my life. It has seen many good times and indeed continues to see them. But it is not the bricks and mortar but the quality of the community that envelopes us. I cannot recall ever having a bad word or even a bad thought about any of my neighbours. Many of them have lived here for as long as I have. I am particularly pleased that another generation of the Beckwith's are living next to me and would particularly like to welcome Peter here today. Ruth – Peter's wife- and Brenda were good pals. Those who were here at the time of the Queens Silver Jubilee in 1977 are not likely to forget that event.

Brenda and Ruth decided that what this community needed was a street party to celebrate the day. As I remember it, there was not the wildest of enthusiasm at first but after Ruth and Brenda worked on them they stirred up a volcano of fervour. They got the police to ban motors from the street. They collected old sheets and dyed them red, white and blue and made bunting from them. They organized the food, celebration mugs, entertainment for children and adults and with considerable foresight arranged for the use of the school in case it rained – and it did.

Well Peter – I expect they are both up there somewhere organizing the pants off someone who believed heaven was a place for rest and relaxation.

And there is dear Rita and Peter Moore. Rita says she looks across at my house every morning when she goes off to work to see if there is some sign of activity. Between her and the milkman they should ensure that I don't moulder away for too long before I am discovered.

And of course there are too many others to mention - but you all make a significant contribution to my well-being. So, I am afraid my neighbours, you are going to have to put up with me for a while longer.

My Liberal Democrat colleagues

Little did I realise what I was letting myself in for when somewhere around 1980 I signed up with them. I thought I would just pay my subscription every year – smile benignly upon their progress – probably even vote for them. But my work for them has given me an aim in life that I would greatly miss and those who were colleagues are now my friends. I was talking the other day to Bruce Routledge – our revered Treasurer. We were discussing a campaign to increase our membership. We decided on a new motto.

"We may not be that good at getting our candidates elected – but we have an awful lot of fun trying"

And finally my family

I suppose the one dark cloud in my 80 years was Brenda's early illness and eventual death. Sad because she was unable to see the full fruition of her devotion to the welfare of her family. Sad because she was not able to share the peace and contentment that retirement and innumerable friendships have granted to me.

I am blessed with three daughters. I am immensely proud of each one of them. Each has developed a family life that is comfortable, caring, interesting and yet very different from the others — yet in each case I am made to feel contented and welcome in their company. And unlike many families they get on so well together. They have married good men and each has brought in- law relationships that have enriched my life.

There is however one thing I have to say to my sons-in- law. Don't you think it is time you injected a bit more urgency into your plans for looking after me in my dotage?

The best offers I have received so far are:
-From Stephen and Lesley — he will tidy out his garage
-From Steve and Jill — well he was going to tow a small boat behind his barge. But now having sold the barge I see nothing forthcoming
-And from Curt and Ali — I can doss down in their veranda and they will even provide me a hot water bottle to protect me against the alpine nights. I have to say though that I would also need a chair lift up to their front door before I could contemplate that offer. So gentlemen, I would like to see a bit more movement in that direction please. I certainly cannot contemplate living in an old people's home, watching daytime television in the common room and having nothing to do but complain about the matron and the food.

Well my friends I would like to propose a toast — in fact, if you can endure it, I would like to propose three. So make sure your glasses are well charged. My wine waiter will pass amongst you and replenish your glasses without spilling too much in your lap.

My first toast is to Brenda and Ruth. I hope they are looking down benignly on this gathering. By the law of averages it will not be too long before Peter and I join you. But I have to say that we are in no hurry.

To Brenda and Ruth!

My second toast it to my newest granddaughter Edie May. Nothing could have been a more wonderful 80th birthday gift than her safe arrival. And again I am reminded of the words from "What a Wonderful World"

> *"I see babies crying. I watch them grow*
> *they'll learn much more that I'll ever know*
> *And I think to myself what a wonderful world"*

To Edie May!

My friends. I think you are the salt of the earth. And I want to propose a toast to each and every one of you. May our comfortable life styles and friendship long continue. Yet may we also continue to bear in mind and to work for those who are perhaps less advantaged than us.

To us all!

Comments:

-Angandshawn   August 07,2010

What a cute speech from your dad! It sounds like he was a great guy, with a fun sense of humor. I'm glad you were able to reconnect with him in a special way this past summer. We look forward to having you back!

-stromqui   August 09, 2010

I have thoroughly enjoyed following your trip and I'm very happy for your accomplishment. You face shows what a wonderful time you've had. It's all a fitting remembrance of your father
Don S

-Linda   August 09, 2010

Ali, dear pal. Your blog has pumped my affinity for England, provided spiritual nourishment, offered up some good laughs and constant smiles. That you are rejuvenated, body and soul, is irresistible. Two months is a tiny investment for such and abundant return. Your accomplishments stir me. Publishing your dad's letter crowns the whole adventure. See ya

Ali, what an incredible accomplishment! Even though I have been stuck in my hammock all summer, I feel like I've gone along with you. You descriptions of the people and places you've seen, the pictures, and the philosophical musings were not only entertaining, but thought provoking and uplifting as well. Thanks so much for blogging about your amazing walk.

10

EPILOGUE

Of course, my journey did not end just over the Scottish border, at Kirk Yetholm. I am still on my journey as we all are, through life. Still on a never-ending quest for happiness and contentment, still growing and developing, trying to reach my full potential –whatever that may be.

Back in the turbulence of my real life, with all its responsibilities and obligations, I find myself questioning what I really did learn from all those miles of walking.

But perhaps I should stop questioning because in all honesty when I let go of trying to get anywhere, in doing so I got there. I think perhaps that is the biggest lesson of all. I have to remember to allow things to unfold rather than forcing things to happen. Less control over my life is better. I have to trust in my intuitions and myself.

My second toe is still longer than my big toe and although I feel far from it most days, I am still the same Queen Boudicca I imagined myself to be in that pub in Cornwall. It is all about how we choose to view ourselves.

I have to admit that everyday I still yearn for that simplistic and calm life back on the trail but I realize I cannot live for yesterday and that true happiness came to me when I stopped wanting and just appreciated my life as I lived it. I will continue to follow my dreams but intend to enjoy all the steps along the way.

"I went to the woods because I wished to live deliberately, to front only the essential facts of life, and to see if I could not learn what it had to teach, and not, when I came to die that I had not lived"
Henry Thoreau

ABOUT THE AUTHOR

Ali is a misplaced English rose living in a snowy cabin in the Rocky Mountains of Utah with her husband Curt, son Ivan, one eyed dog Ruby and a ferret named Fritz. She works as a nurse in the Fatigue Consultation Clinic in Salt lake City and in her spare time, skis, bikes, hikes and occasionally goes for a very long walk. She hopes this book will help other ordinary people realize they are capable of extra-ordinary things.

Made in the USA
Lexington, KY
01 September 2017